Executive editor
Campbell L. Goldsmid
Editor Jean Cooke
Text by
Peter Robson
Theodore Rowland-Entwistle
Designer Jenny Frith
Picture Research
Brian Cotton

SBN 361 04649 9
Copyright © Autumn Publishing
1980
Published 1980 by Purnell Books,
Berkshire House, Queen Street,
Maidenhead, Berkshire

Designed and produced for Purnell
Books by Autumn Publishing Ltd,
10 Eastgate Square, Chichester,
Sussex

Made and printed by Purnell and
Sons Ltd., Paulton, Bristol

The Book of
GREAT ESCAPES

Based on True Life Stories!

Purnell

CONTENTS

INTRODUCTION

Captain James Lovell

Since the beginning of time Man has possessed a sense of adventure. To seek out the unknown and explore new horizons or accomplish the unusual—this has been Man's drive to satisfy thirst for knowledge and provide a feeling of achievement.

'Space' was that adventure for me. During my career in the US Space Program I made four flights into space, including two flights to the Moon. At one time I held the record for time in space. The real satisfaction, however, was to do something Man had not done before—in my case, to become the first person to orbit the Moon. It was Christmas Eve, 1968, when Apollo Eight started its orbit around the Moon. Bill Anders, Frank Borman and myself were like three tourists with our faces pressed to the window looking at the ancient craters below. I will never forget viewing the Earth rise above the lunar horizon.

Adventure always brings the unexpected. Suddenly Man is faced with overwhelming odds. This is the time when raw courage, initiative, perhaps some strategy and always a little luck are required to provide a happy ending. That time came for me on Apollo Thirteen. An explosion on our spacecraft almost marooned me in space. You will find the adventure of my 'Great Escape' back to Earth in the pages of this book.

In fact, this book is filled with the perilous situations people find themselves in and their 'Great Escapes' from Man or the elements. Read on and relive their exciting, true-life adventures.

WE'VE GOT A PROBLEM

Apollo 13's escape from disaster

Sun-god emblem of Apollo 13.

It was 13.13 hours Houston Time on Saturday April 13, 1970, when the spacecraft *Apollo 13* blasted off on the US National Aeronautics and Space Administration's third manned lunar mission. After the excitement and publicity surrounding many previous space projects, *Apollo 13*'s task was generally regarded as almost routine. Its object was little more than a geological survey of the lunar mountains.

The spacecraft was manned by US Navy officer Captain James A. Lovell, the commander, together with lunar module pilot Fred W. Haise and command module pilot John L. Swigert. Early on Tuesday *Apollo 13* was well on course to the Moon, 330,000 kilometres (205,000 miles) away from Earth. It was virtually the point of no return, but the entire mission had been so uneventful that a television programme beamed back to Earth on Monday showing the crew at work had so far been ignored by US television channels. Lovell had signed off the programme with 'This is the crew of *Apollo 13* wishing everyone down there a nice evening.'

Then a few minutes later

Blast-off: the Saturn V rocket lifting Apollo 13 into space for what was to prove the most dangerous Moon mission of all.

Mission Control's radio linkman at Houston, Texas, Jack Lousma, heard Swigert's voice say: 'Hey! We've got a problem here . . .'

It was the understatement of all time, and it sparked off one of the world's most expensive, desperate and seemingly impossible rescue attempts—for an explosion had shaken the spacecraft.

On board *Apollo 13*, Lovell and Swigert thought at first that the explosion was one of Fred Haise's jokes. They had heard something similar when he operated a valve in the lunar landing module. But the astonishment on Haise's face proved that the incident was nothing to do with him.

Swigert checked the gauges on the console before him in the control module. Everything appeared to be functioning normally, but when Haise returned from examining the lunar module and Swigert glanced again at the gauges ranged before him he realised that they were in trouble. Two oxygen pressure gauges were dropping at an alarming rate. One fuel tank had failed completely and another was giving out. Lovell and his colleagues realised that their command module would soon be totally dead. That explosion had damaged both oxygen tanks and caused the

failure of all three main fuel cells. When Mission Control was informed of the damage the Moon landing was instantly abandoned, but everybody concerned knew that bringing Lovell, Haise and Swigert safely back to Earth was going to be no easy task. The damage had caused a drastic reduction in the air supply. There was also a substantial power failure which would seriously hinder supplying electricity to power the command module. It also meant that no water could be made to top up the ration in the tanks.

One of the three fuel cells functioned for about two hours. Then, when Fred Haise reported that the oxygen pressure was dropping in the control cabin, Mission Control replied: 'We're starting to think about the Lunar Module lifeboat.'

Back came the reply from *Apollo 13*: 'Yes, that's something we're thinking about, too.'

It had dawned on the crew and Mission Control alike that the only hope of preventing the spacecraft from cruising indefinitely into space was to use the lunar landing module—that part of the spacecraft designed to land on the Moon—as a 'lifeboat'. Its power systems and supplies could swing the crippled spacecraft around the Moon in an orbit

The army of controllers at the Kennedy Space Centre in Florida have all eyes on the screen at take-off time. It took a team this size to monitor every aspect of a Moon-flight.

Chain of errors

A chain of errors caused the *Apollo 13* disaster. The first was that the switches in the service module's oxygen tank were designed for use at 28 volts—and they had to cope with 65 volts. Luckily similar switches had stood the extra voltage on earlier missions.

Then the oxygen tank was dropped during assembly and a bit of tubing inside it came loose. As a result the oxygen in it could not be removed in the usual way during pre-flight preparations. Heat and high pressure were used to force it out—and the voltage used fused the switches.

Those switches were designed to cut out when there was any overheating. There *was* overheating, which led to a short-circuit in a fan motor—and then came the explosion.

As the crew finally saw it: the damaged service module of Apollo 13 drifts away after it is jettisoned. An entire panel on the spacecraft was blown away by the explosion.

towards the narrow 'space corridor', leading the *Apollo* crew safely back to Earth.

One and a half hours after the crisis began, Mission Control told *Apollo 13*: 'We figure that there is just about 15 minutes' worth of power left in the command module. So we want you to start getting over in the LM and getting some power on that.'

Fred Haise and James Lovell were already working in the lunar module, and shortly before six o'clock on Tuesday morning Jack Swigert joined them. The command module was temporarily abandoned.

There was still a serious problem. The spacecraft faced a journey of almost four days, and

unless every effort was made to save power, oxygen and water, the lunar module's supplies would only last for less than half that time.

An hour later, technicians and astronauts in flight simulators at Mission Control were working flat out to solve the problems that were to be overcome for those on *Apollo 13* during the next few days. At 9.30 that same morning, Lovell received instructions for the first rocket burn that would alter the spacecraft's course. It was carried out perfectly.

A more crucial burn was also performed skilfully at 3.30 on Wednesday morning, and radio contact was lost as the spacecraft vanished on the far side of the Moon. As those on Earth waited more anxiously than usual for radio contact to be restored, *Apollo* came out from behind the Moon, precisely placed on course for Earth. Ninety

minutes later, however, James Lovell's voice calmly informed Mission Control that they faced another very serious problem. The air-conditioning system was not working properly and poisonous carbon dioxide fumes were reaching dangerous levels.

The technicians and Houston-based astronauts worked quickly to resolve this crisis, too. The result was a life-saving, do-it-yourself air-scrubbing unit, which Lovell, Swigert and Haise could put together with equipment that was already on board *Apollo 13.*

It was a slow task for them, working in cold and poor light, but slowly they assembled the scrubbing unit by connecting a lithium hydroxide canister to the air supply with spare hoses from their spacesuits.

No sooner had this problem been overcome than Mission Control spotted another high-risk hazard. While the crew had been securing their air supply *Apollo 13* had drifted further off course than any other Moon-flight. On its present course it would miss the Earth and was again in danger of becoming lost in space.

Another critical rocket burn was needed, but James Lovell —who had flown more space miles than any other astronaut—was so in command of the situation that he managed a couple of hours' sleep before returning to the controls. Then at 5.31 on Thursday morning, before altering course, he remarked wryly to Houston: 'Well, I hope you guys in the back room have thought this up right.'

Lovell had no need to worry. At the moment of the third burn, the NASA technicians had already worked out the complex manoeuvres that would be needed to help bring *Apollo 13* back into the Earth's atmosphere the following day. And these were being checked and double-checked in flight simulators by the *Apollo 14* crew, astronauts Alan Shepherd, Stuart Roosa and Edgar Mitchell.

It was 1.53 pm on Friday when Lovell fired the final 23-second rocket burn that swung

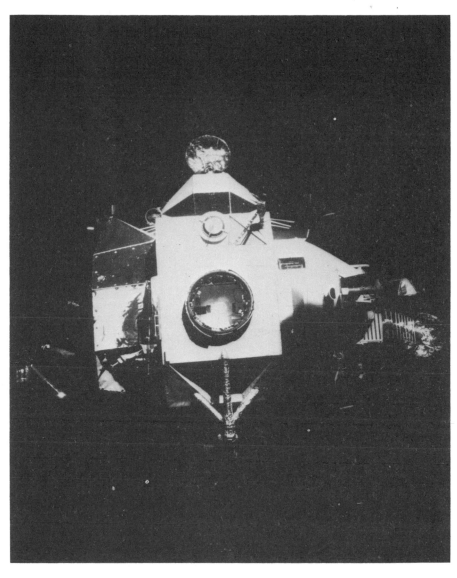

The 'lifeboat' that saved the Apollo 13 crew: the lunar module, photographed from the command module just after it too had been jettisoned. The module, codenamed 'Aquarius', spun off into space after it was abandoned.

voice from Houston said almost in relief: 'That's the end of the age of Aquarius for *Apollo 13*.'

Just over an hour later the command module crashed into the Earth's atmosphere at the end of an incredible journey and for several minutes Mission Control again lost contact. But *Apollo 13* was heading safely home.

At 7.07 pm the command module splashed triumphantly down in the Pacific Ocean less than six kilometres (four miles) away from the waiting rescue ship *Iwo Jima*. And despite their three-and-a-half-day ordeal, with the threat of being marooned in space, James Lovell was able to report to Mission Control: 'We're in good shape.'

Safe at last: the command module parachutes safely into the South Pacific after the greatest escape ever.

the crippled *Apollo* into the correct re-entry position, several hours before entering the Earth's atmosphere. The damaged service module, which carried the oxygen tanks and other supplies, was jettisoned to expose the vital heatshield needed to protect the craft during re-entry. For the first time, the crew saw the extent of the damage. Lovell reported to Mission Control at Houston: 'There is one whole side of the thing missing—almost from the base to the engine.' Viewers on Earth gasped when they saw how badly *Apollo 13* had been crippled by the explosion.

At 5.44 pm the life-saving lunar landing module was also jettisoned. James Lovell was the last to leave that section for the command module. As *Aquarius* —the codename for the lunar module—spun off into space, a

THE GREAT HOUDINI

Escaper extraordinary

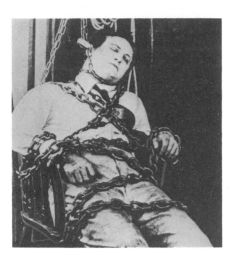

In a crowded Berlin court-room in 1906 dozens of people, including the judge, jury, lawyers and court officials, watched an amazing demonstration which was being offered as evidence in a libel case. Police chief Werner Graff slapped a gleaming new pair of specially-constructed handcuffs on a small, lithely-built man who stood before the court. Then, with the help of several policemen, Graff bound the man with a series of steel chains, each one fastened about him with its own padlock.

By the time that stage of the exercise had been finished, all that could be seen of their victim was his head, peering out at the court-room over an entwined mass of locks and chains. Werner Graff stepped back triumphantly, tossed his bundle of padlock keys to another police officer and said to the shackled man: 'Now, let's see what you can do to escape from that!'

His victim was the Great Houdini, world-famous as an escapologist, and once again about to demonstrate his skill. Werner Graff had publicly denounced Houdini as a fake during the magician's sensational tour of Germany. So Houdini had taken the police chief to court, claiming damages for libel. Graff happily accepted Houdini's challenge to place him in an 'escape-proof' situation in the court.

Nobody expected Houdini to prove Graff wrong. Yet within five minutes the Great Houdini had astonished everybody in that courtroom. For the chains, padlocks and even the special hand-

cuffs all fell from his body to the floor—amid resounding cheers.

During Houdini's lifetime, and even after his death in 1926, there were countless claims by people that he was an impostor and a fake, but he was undoubtedly a supreme showman. His stunts and challenges made him a very wealthy man, and his expertise happily mystified his delighted public.

Although Houdini claimed

Harry Houdini was one of the greatest magicians ever, and a superb showman.

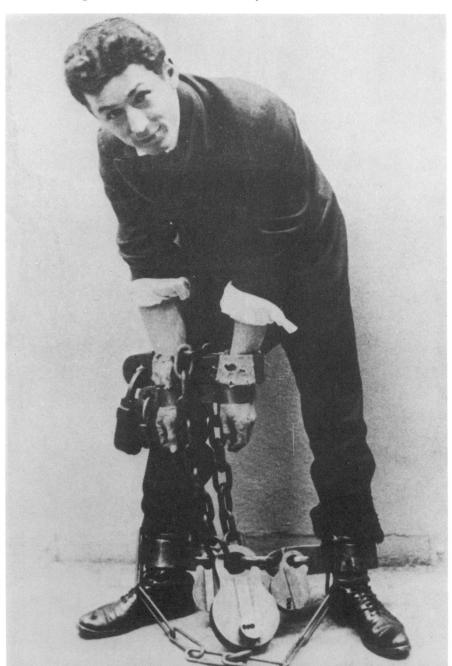

Houdini in heavy manacles and leg-irons just before one of his fabulous escapes.

to have been born Harry Houdini at Appleton, Wisconsin, on March 24, 1874, the only truth in that statement was his date of birth. His real name was Erich Weiss and his father had been a rabbi in Budapest, in Hungary, who emigrated to the United States. When he became a professional magician, young Weiss adopted the name Houdini after a great French magician, Jean Robert-Houdin, who had died in 1871.

Houdini began his show-business career as a circus acrobat. This work made him a magnificent athlete. He was also a naturally brilliant mechanic, and he had an almost yoga-like control over his body. All of this certainly helped Houdini to make himself into a legend in his own lifetime.

During his astonishing career he challenged more than twelve police forces to prevent him from escaping from situations of their own choosing. On each occasion Houdini's 'magic' proved unbeatable.

In Washington's federal jail he was locked without his clothes in a cell in the notorious Murderers' Row. Houdini slipped free from his manacles and opened the cell door within five minutes. Then he speedily opened all the other cells, moved the convicts around him like human pawns on a chessboard, and finally appeared fully-dressed in the warden's office.

In San Francisco Houdini was shackled naked to a cell wall by a senior police official and the jail warden. They barely had time to return to the warden's office, light their cigars and settle down, before Houdini knocked on the office door. Again he was fully dressed, with the opened manacles dangling from one hand, a lighted cigar nonchalantly and elegantly held in the other.

One of Houdini's more bizarre escapades happened in St.

One of Houdini's most spectacular feats—wriggling out of a strait-jacket while suspended upside-down from a New York skyscraper. As usual, he escaped with ease.

Petersburg (now Leningrad), when he accepted a challenge from Imperial Russia's dreaded secret police, the Ochrana. The Ochrana used steel-walled, escape-proof prison wagons, called cassettes, to transport prisoners to Siberia. The cassettes were virtually impregnable. There was only a small barred window high up on one side, 125 millimetres (5

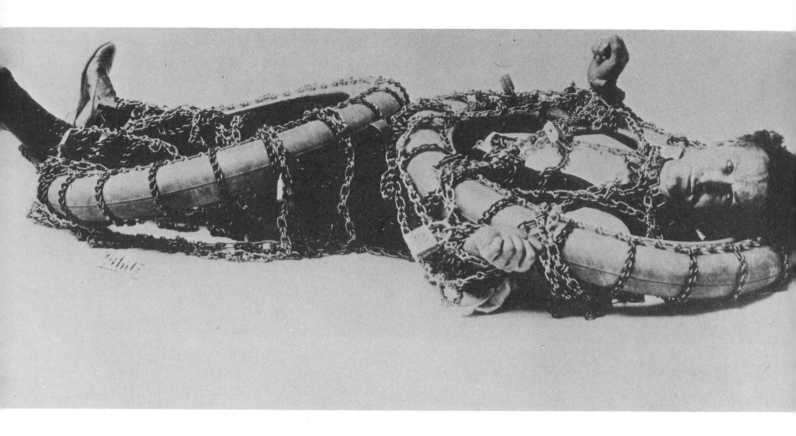

inches) square, and one solid steel door that was locked, bolted and chained from the outside.

A very special cassette was prepared to imprison Houdini. It was equipped with extra locks, bolts and chains. One cold winter's morning Houdini was escorted out into the prison yard. The Ochrana officers stripped him, then searched him for concealed tools and implements. Next he was handcuffed and shackled in leg irons before being placed inside the cassette, which was securely sealed. Houdini's clothes were placed in a neat bundle a few yards away.

Less than an hour later the Ochrana officers were sitting round a warm stove in their office when Houdini knocked at the door. He was fully dressed and had apparently pulled off another incredible escape. When the officers checked the cassette it was still chained, locked and bolted, precisely as it had been when they placed the manacled Houdini inside.

Nothing, it seemed, was too outrageous for Harry Houdini to tackle. Among his many other spectacular demonstrations was hanging upside down from the top of a New York skyscraper, lashed into a strait-jacket. He escaped. On another occasion he was stripped, handcuffed by police, and pushed through a hole cut in the thick ice covering the Detroit River. Six agonising minutes—during which people fainted, screamed and became hysterical —passed before Houdini, wet and shivering, was seen clambering back to safety.

Off-stage, too, he demonstrated incredible physical strength and agility. Several people witnessed him, in private, tying some knots in a piece of string during an after-dinner conversation. Then, removing his shoes and socks, he would sit back and almost absent-mindedly unpick the knots with his toes.

His death was due to his showmanship. Houdini loved demonstrating that he could never be injured by even the heaviest blow to his stomach. But on October 22, 1926, he was visited in Montreal by some college students. One of them slammed a heavy blow to Houdini's belly before the illusionist had time to tense his abdominal muscles in preparation. Houdini became seriously ill with an inflamed

The man nothing could hold— not even this collection of chains and padlocks.

appendix, but insisted on appearing on stage that night. Peritonitis set in, and he died on October 31, aged only 52.

The magic secret

How did Harry Houdini perform his amazing feats? Like all magicians, he kept his secrets to himself. But he had an assistant, William (Jim) Collins, who used to check the cells and apparatus before Houdini allowed himself to be shackled and locked up.

Though he was stripped and searched, people never looked at the soles of his feet—and it is said that he used to tape a piece of wire there, which he could use to pick locks. Above all, he had superb physical control; he could flex his muscles when he was being tied up, so when he relaxed his bonds loosened.

THE JAWS OF DEATH

Escape from a killer shark

In the silent, green underwater world of South Australia's Aldinga Reef, 23-year-old Rodney Fox swam cautiously around a large rock and saw that the morwong fish was still there, nibbling at a clump of weed. Smiling to himself beneath his face-mask, he started aiming his spear-gun at the fish. It was a large morwong—heavy enough, perhaps, to tip the results of the South Australian Skin-Diving and Spear-Fishing championship in his favour.

Suddenly—a second before he could fire—something surged powerfully through the sea towards him, smashing into his left shoulder and carrying him off at an astonishing speed. Rodney's mask was ripped from his face by the shock of the attack, the spear gun was knocked from his hand and there was such pressure gripping his body that he felt as if he

Rodney Fox leaving the water after an earlier dive.

was being crushed in some gigantic fist. Then he twisted round and realised with blood-chilling fear that he had been seized by one of the world's most ferocious and predatory sea monsters: a white killer shark.

Ironically, a few hours earlier on that warm Sunday morning in 1963 Rodney had promised his wife Kay that this would be the last occasion on which he would compete in the championship. The monster of the deep looked as if it was going to make that promise one which would be impossible to break. Rodney had already won the title in the 1961-62 contest and had been runner up the following year. He had spent months training for the 1963-64 competition.

Each competitor was a free-diver, and swam without the help of breathing equipment. Rodney had trained himself to dive as far as 30 metres (100 feet) and

Rodney Fox with a 4·25-metre (14-foot) shark which he landed off Port Lincoln.

remain there for more than a minute. Every precaution was taken to guard against sharks. Two powerful motor-launches, carrying skilled marksmen, were patrolling the contest area constantly looking out for the killers. The lesser sharks, such as the bronze whaler and the grey, were more of a nuisance than a danger; they seldom attacked skin-divers, but they drove the fish away. The great white sharks rarely came close enough. As an added precaution, each of the 40 spearfishermen had a long line fastened to his weighted belt, which was attached to a hollow float that remained on the surface. The moment a fish was speared, it was placed in the float to prevent its blood contaminating the sea and attracting the prowling killer sharks to the area.

The contest had started at nine o'clock that morning. Round about noon, with two hours remaining, Rodney Fox swam ashore, towing the laden float to add the fish it contained to his catch piled up on the shore. He reckoned he had more than 27 kilogrammes (60 lb)—parrot fish, snoek, snapper and magpie perch —which was considerably more than almost anybody else.

Returning to the sea, he swam out for more than 1.6 kilometres (a mile) searching for bigger fish. On the way back to the shore, earlier that morning, he remembered, he had spotted some morwong fish feeding close to a large, curiously shaped rock. He succeeded in locating the rock again and saw that one morwong was still lurking there.

Rodney approached cautiously, swimming further out to sea before diving and then making his approach behind cover of the rock. Perhaps the great white shark had followed him in from the sea, but certainly the moment he was about to fire his steel-shafted barb, it attacked.

Its powerful jaws gripped his chest; his left shoulder was well down in its throat. Frantically, before his breath gave out, Rodney Fox fought for his life. He lashed back at the monstrous head with his hand, reaching to gouge out the shark's eyes. For a second, the shark relaxed its grip.

Rodney pushed out with his hands to escape, and the mons-

ter's razor-sharp teeth snapped down and seized his right arm. Almost fainting with pain, he fought and kicked and wrenched himself free. Shooting to the surface as rapidly as he could, Rodney realised that the killer shark was still hunting him, lusting after the blood trailing from the wounds all over his body and arm. He twisted desperately to avoid its gaping jaws as it followed him all the way to the surface.

Bursting out of the sea, Rodney Fox sucked in lungs-full of air, so stunned by the attack that he was unable to call for help. Then he saw the fin slicing through the sea towards him again. The shark dived to attack and its hard body brushed past. Gulping down as much air as he could, Rodney suddenly dived for the shark as it spun round to attack him again. It missed and he wrapped himself round its body, clinging with his arms and legs as it dragged him down to the depths of the sea.

The great white shark twisted furiously, trying to shake Rodney off. Then, with his lungs almost bursting, Rodney released his tenacious grip and kicked for the surface again. As his head

surfaced, he saw that all around him the sea was red with blood —*his* blood.

A few yards away the sea seemed to boil angrily as the shark followed him, intent on renewing the attack. Rodney knew that his strength was fast ebbing away with his blood. He could not fight much longer against such a relentless killer.

Yet incredibly the shark struck blindly. Swerving just before lunging at Rodney it seized his hollow fish float, and became caught up in the long line that linked the float with his belt. Baffled, the shark dived, trying to release itself. Rodney struggled to unbuckle the belt as he, too, was dragged down, thinking: 'My God! I'm not going to drown. . . not now. . .'

The line broke beneath the strain, Rodney shot back to the surface and yelled: 'Shark! Shark! Shark!'

The alarm was on. He saw the patrol launches skimming across the bay towards him, and prayed that the killer shark would not attack again before he could be rescued. In minutes the launches reached him. Friendly strong hands reached down and plucked him from the blood-stained sea. Somebody was saying: 'Hang on, mate! Hang on, it's over . . . we've got you now.'

Rodney Fox had not escaped lightly from his horrifying ordeal. His right arm and hand were so badly mangled that the bones were exposed in several places. His chest, back, shoulder and side had been so badly savaged and torn that his rescuers could clearly see his rib-cage and lungs. Practically all that was holding his body together, it seemed, was the remains of his rubber skin-diving suit. An ambulance rushed him 55 kilometres (34 miles) for emergency treatment at hospital in Adelaide, with police holding back all the traffic at the highway intersections until the ambulance raced past.

Today, Rodney Fox still bears grim mementoes of his escape from the killer white shark. There are still scars on his chest and back, while his right hand shows where it was badly mangled. Yet a mere five months afterwards he returned to skin-diving, to overcome the terrible memories of the day that he so narrowly escaped a dreadful death—though he now stays well away from places where sharks are likely to lurk.

'The great white shark had followed him in . . . the moment he was about to fire his steel-shafted barb, it attacked. Its powerful jaws gripped his chest and his left shoulder.'

THE ROYAL OAK
Charles II's escape after the Battle

Charles II in later life: from an engraving made during his lifetime. He is wearing a wig.

Through the twilight of a September day a party of sixty or so weary, dishevelled men rode through the quiet countryside of Worcestershire. They had but two thoughts: to escape from the danger that lay all around them in this apparently harmless landscape, and to preserve the safety of a tall, dark-haired, swarthy young man who rode in their midst. For the year was 1651, and the young man was the 21-year-old Charles Stuart, whom royalist Englishmen regarded as Charles II, King of England since his father, Charles I, was executed in January 1649. And Charles II, trying to win back his kingdom, had just been crushingly defeated by the Ironsides of Oliver Cromwell at the Battle of Worcester.

There was only one thing for it, Charles decided: the party must split up. With the coming of dawn they reached a manor house called White Ladies, where the King was able to rest, and have some food and drink. Most of his followers wanted to go to Scotland, where they thought there would be safety, and where they could carry on the fight. Charles was more realistic and knew that for the moment all was lost. He decided to make for London, where he could find a ship to take him to France, and to go alone. Only one of his followers, Lord Wilmot, was to remain in touch.

The tenant of White Ladies was John Penderel, who looked after the estate. He was loyal to the Stuart cause. John had four brothers, William, Richard, Humphrey and George, and the five Penderels took the fugitive King in their charge. First of all they provided him with a change of clothes—a rough shirt, a greasy leather hat and waistcoat, a worn green coat, grey breeches, and rough, ill-fitting shoes. Richard Penderel then led him into a little wood, where he hid all day in pouring rain while parties of Roundhead soldiers rode by, looking for fugitive Cavaliers fleeing from the disaster of Worcester.

A Royalist supporter bringing food to Charles as he sheltered in a barn, in rough clothes.

That night, after a brief call for food at the cottage where Richard Penderel and his widowed mother lived, Charles and Richard set off on foot towards Wales, where the King thought it would be easier to find a ship than in London. It was a long trudge, during which they were chased by a miller who thought they were thieves, and by midnight the King was worn out. His feet were blistered and bleeding because his shoes fitted him so badly. They found refuge for the coming day in a barn belonging to a royalist sympathiser.

The way to Wales was barred by the River Severn, which it was impossible to cross undetected. So next night Charles and his loyal follower set off back towards White Ladies. On the way they came to a river, which was swollen by rain.

'Now we are undone—I can't swim,' said Richard Penderel.

'But I can,' said the King. 'It's only a little river—I'll help you over.'

A few minutes later, wet but safe, they were on the other side. This time they went to Boscobel, home of William, the eldest of the Penderel brothers. There they found another Royalist fugitive, Major William Carlis. The next

'The King climbed into a huge, leafy oak tree ... and spent all day in safety while parties of Roundheads searched the woods all around.'

day, at Carlis's suggestion, he and the King climbed into a huge, leafy oak tree, with food, drink and a cushion, and there Charles slept all day in safety, while parties of Roundheads searched the woods all around them.

The following day it was found to be safe for the King to rest at Boscobel, and then, riding a slow, ambling work-horse belonging to Humphrey Penderel, Charles made his way to

the house of another Royalist, escorted by the five faithful brothers. When Charles commented on the sluggishness of the horse, Humphrey said with a grin: 'Can you blame the horse for going slowly when he has the weight of three kingdoms on his back?'—a reference to Charles's titles as king of England, Scotland and Ireland.

Among these new friends fresh plans were made for Charles's escape. A few days later he was trotting along in a suit of sober grey, disguised as William Jackson, a servant in attendance on a girl named Jane Lane, who rode pillion on the horse behind him. At one point on their week's journey the horse cast a shoe, and the pretended servant had to take it to the nearest smithy. There the blacksmith, a staunch Puritan, commented that several Royalists were taken, but not that rogue Charles Stuart. 'If that rogue's taken he deserves to be hanged,' said the disguised King with great cheerfulness.

Jane Lane was visiting a friend near Bristol, where the King hoped to find a boat. There was a nasty moment when the butler of the house, named Pope, recognised Charles, but Pope proved a loyal friend and did his best to find a ship for him. It was necessary for the King to move

elsewhere, but having just arrived, how was Jane to cut short her visit without arousing suspicion? Pope and the King put their heads together, and concocted a letter saying that Jane's father was dangerously ill. Pope solemnly handed it over, and within a few hours Jane and her pretended servant were on their travels again.

Next the King sought refuge with an old friend, Colonel Frank Wyndham, at Trent House in Dorset. There he lay hidden in

The King, disguised as a servant, with Jane Lane riding pillion behind him.

great comfort for two long weeks, his presence known to only five people in a household of 20. One day he heard the church bells, and learned that one of Cromwell's troopers was there, claiming he had personally killed the malignant Charles Stuart. The villagers were ringing the bells and lighting the bonfires to celebrate the news.

While Charles rested, Frank Wyndham made arrangements for a ship to take Charles over to France. His friend Lord Wilmot, who had been travelling round the country completely undisguised, was to go with him. Once more the King became the servant Will Jackson. This time Juliana Coningsby, a pretty young cousin of Frank Wyndham, was his pillion passenger. They rode to the little Dorset village of Charmouth, where Juliana and Wilmot posed as a pair of eloping lovers, with 'Will Jackson' to wait on them. But there was no boat waiting for them at Charmouth.

Colonel Wyndham's mother receiving the refugee King at Trent House in Dorset.

While they were pondering what to do a new peril arose. The local blacksmith became suspicious, and after some trouble aroused a Puritan minister, Benjamin Wesley. They alerted a troop of Roundhead soldiers, who found that the supposed lovers and their servant had left for Bridport. Off rode the soldiers in hot pursuit. But luckily the King and his companions had turned off the main road. After many wanderings they returned to Trent House, where the King waited another anxious week while fresh plans were laid. Wyndham got in contact with some Royalists at Salisbury, who set about finding another ship.

Soon Charles was off again,

'His short hair led his host to take him for a Roundhead.'

this time to Heale House near Salisbury, where he spent five days in a secret hiding place. Many large English houses had such secret places, often known as 'priest's holes' because priests of the then banned Roman Catholic religion used to be concealed there. Charles had already spent a day in such a hidden chamber at one of the houses he was staying in, while Roundhead soldiers were threatening to search the house. From Heale House Charles rode to a house at Hambledon, a small town where people were beginning to play a game with bat and ball, later to be known as cricket. Though his companions, among them Lord Wilmot, were known to be Royalists, the King was still disguised, and his short cropped hair led his host, Thomas Symons, to take him for a Round-

head. However, Symons settled down to drink with the company in a convivial style, occasionally addressing the King as 'Brother Roundhead'. Charles responded to the supposed character and whenever Symons loosed a drunken oath, he would say very piously, 'Oh, dear brother, swear not, I beseech you!'

Next day the little party rode over to a small fishing village called Brighthelmstone (now the huge town of Brighton), where another Royalist, Colonel George Gounter, had at last persuaded a ship's captain to take a Royalist fugitive to France. At 7 a.m. on October 15 the ship slid out of a little creek where she had been lying, and Charles sailed away to France—and safety. He did not regain his throne until nine years later.

REAL-LIFE BEAU GESTE

Barry Galvin's escape from the Foreign Legion

Barry Galvin after his escape from the French Foreign Legion.

Head shaven, Barry Galvin does punishment for a minor offence. Discipline in the Foreign Legion was extremely harsh.

The slim, sun-tanned young Legionnaire standing outside a small café in Bonifacio, Corsica, appeared to be simply giving directions to an Englishwoman who looked for all the world like just another tourist. The truth of the matter was quite different. The woman was Mrs. Sadie Galvin, and the young Legionnaire was her son Barry. It was the first time in almost two years that they had set eyes on each other. They could risk chatting for only a few moments, but it was long enough for Sadie Galvin to start planning one of the most determined escapes from that famous, but ruthless, regiment of mercenary soldiers, the French Foreign Legion.

Like so many other young men, Barry left his home in Addleston, Surrey, because he wanted a more adventurous life. He was turned down by the British army, so he went to France to find out how easy it was to follow in the fictional footsteps of the hero of P.C. Wren's novel about the Legion, *Beau Geste*. It proved all too easy. When Barry arrived at Lille, where there was a Legion recruitment office, he met a Legionnaire who took him to a cheap hostel where he could spend the night. The next morning when Barry awoke he found that the hostel's 'registration documents' which he had signed had actually enrolled him into the Legion. An officer offered to destroy the documents if Barry felt like changing his mind, but Barry agreed to give the famous Legion a trial. It was a decision he was soon to regret.

The 19-year-old Englishman was sent to Corsica for his basic training. He climbed out of a truck at the barracks there, with other recruits, straight into the traditional Foreign Legion welcome: a sergeant punched him in the face. More than 50 French Foreign Legion recruits started the same day as Barry Galvin. After the four months' basic training had been completed fewer than half remained. Some had been injured or killed on the training course, some had been beaten to death by their comrades for stealing, some had escaped, unable to stand Legion life, and some had committed suicide.

The Legion's 'crash course' in fluent French was as brutal as it was effective. French was the language of the Legion: to understand orders Legionnaires had to understand French. So those who could not speak the language were lined up on the parade ground, in full uniform, beneath the blazing Corsican mid-day sun. They stood to attention reading through a French dictionary. If they had not committed 100 words to memory within two hours, they remained in position there all night as punishment.

Barry's mother had been trying to trace him ever since he had disappeared. She first knew he had joined the French Foreign Legion when she received a postcard from a stranger, who had spoken briefly to Barry during a holiday in Corsica. Barry had asked the stranger to let his mother know where he was, because it was quite impossible for Legionnaires to post letters home. It was even more difficult for Legionnaires to be seen speaking to anybody connected with their family. Barry explained to his mother at that first meeting in Bonifacio that Legionnaires were kept under surveillance and reports were filed at headquarters: any who were suspected of planning or attempting to escape were severely punished.

Sadie Galvin promised to do everything she could to help her son escape from the Legion, but first she had to return to England. For the next two months she worked to earn extra money to build inside an old car a secret compartment in which Barry could hide.

Although she kept her escape preparations as secret as possible, because she was worried in case the news reached the French Embassy in London, Sadie had help from a Swiss-born nurse to work out an escape route. The plan was to hide Barry in the car, then catch a ferry from Corsica to Sardinia. Sardinia was Italian territory, which meant that Barry would be safe from the French authorities. The plan seemed foolproof, but the escape failed. After Sadie Galvin collected Barry at a pre-arranged rendezvous, she drove to the ferry terminal—only to discover that for the first time that year the ten a.m. ferry had been withdrawn.

Punishments in the Foreign Legion, Barry found, were as ingenious as they were sadistic. This one required the offender to run up a steep sandbank with a heavy suitcase held in the mouth and a full kitbag grasped in each hand.

A triumphant Sadie Galvin opens the secret compartment to reveal Barry, still in uniform.

It was a bitter blow. There was not another ferry to Sardinia until that afternoon and Barry, who was afraid his absence would be noticed, hurried back to barracks. Sadie Galvin promised to return from Sardinia a week later, collect Barry again and catch the afternoon ferry. But the following week there was no sign of her son at the meeting-place. Instead, another British-born Legionnaire warned her that Barry had been sent to a Legion jail 112 kilometres (70 miles) away: his abortive escape plan had been discovered.

In desperation Sadie Galvin managed to get an interview with her son's commanding officer, who denied that Barry was in prison. The officer agreed to give Barry permission to write home regularly, but told Mrs. Galvin that Barry had been posted to the Comoro Islands, 8,000 kilometres (5,000 miles) away in the Indian Ocean. When Sadie later received

a letter from Barry confirming his posting, she realized that as far as any escape was concerned, the Comoro Islands might as well have been on the dark side of the Moon.

Yet she was determined to continue the fight to free her son from the French Foreign Legion. She launched a publicity campaign in the newspapers, and wrote constantly to both the British and French governments pressing for her son's release. Nobody appeared able to help. Nobody, that was, apart from Frank Withy, a 70-year-old former French Legionnaire living in Sussex. Frank Withy wrote to Sadie Galvin to say that if the opportunity ever came he was certain his experience could help to rescue her son.

Several months later, in the summer of 1976, Sadie Galvin received a letter from Barry in which he explained that he had returned to Corsica for a spell before being transferred to French Guiana. A few days later Barry telephoned home. Sadie Galvin used those few minutes on

the telephone to tell Barry that a second escape attempt would be made, and they arranged a rendezvous at Porto Vecchio, a little Corsican town close to his barracks.

Frank Withy was standing by with an old ambulance, which had been converted into a caravanette. It had a special hiding-place for Barry built beneath one of the bunk-beds. Sadie Galvin and Frank Withy had arranged to meet Barry at noon on August 17 in Porto Vecchio, so they left home in the converted ambulance in what should have been ample time on Saturday, August 14.

Unfortunately, their vehicle met with so many breakdowns that they trundled into Porto Vecchio with only minutes to spare. They parked in a hospital car-park, where the shape of the caravanette would not be too conspicuous. Sadie Galvin heard the rear doors click and knew that Barry was on board. Then, as Frank started up the engine for the journey home, Sadie Galvin made a decision that may well have changed their whole future. She told Frank Withy to go back the way they had come—through France.

Fate played into their hands when they arrived at the dockside in Calais more than 24 hours later. Customs officials were searching every car waiting for the Dover ferry. Sadie Galvin looked at Frank, who was slumped white-faced and exhausted across the steering wheel after what had been a marathon drive for a 70-year-old man. Thinking quickly, she told the French Customs officers that 'her uncle' was very ill. They waved the vehicle through and on to the ferry without searching it.

From the moment the old ambulance left Porto Vecchio until it landed at Dover, Barry remained in hiding. Then at Dover, during a routine drugs search, he was discovered by an astonished Customs Officer—still dressed in his Foreign Legion uniform.

THE PISCES DISASTER

Escape from the depths

Roger Mallinson and Roger Chapman leaned back and relaxed with relief as the mother-ship *Vickers Voyager* started winching in their two-man submarine *Pisces III*. They were on the surface of the cold, grey Atlantic, off the Irish coast, at the end of another routine operation—eight hours of cable-laying 230 fathoms (420 metres) down on the sea bed. It was a tough job, but both men were veterans, with many hundreds of hours' service in submarines behind them.

Then suddenly, just after nine o'clock on that Wednesday morning, August 29, 1973, things went wrong.

Mallinson and Chapman felt *Pisces III* lurch heavily backwards, and start sinking, tail-first. A rear hatch cover had broken loose and water was flooding into the aft section.

Almost before they had time to prepare themselves *Pisces III* plunged 32 fathoms (58 metres), the full length of the hawser that linked it to *Vickers Voyager*. For a few seconds the hawser held. Mallinson and Chapman sprang into action and released their lead ballast, hoping that the loss of its

Roger Chapman gives a cheery wave after his rescue.

Divers and rescue craft join in the search for *Pisces III*, attached by a line to the *Vickers Voyager*.

weight would prevent the line from snapping. But they were too late. The cable parted, and the mini-sub started to gather speed toward the bottom of the sea.

Stowed away in a box on board *Pisces III* were pieces of white rag, intended for cleaning machinery. Mallinson and Chapman grabbed a handful each and stuffed it between their teeth, to save them from biting their tongues when the sub hit the bottom. Moments later, bruised and shocked, with *Pisces III* resting on the ocean floor, they looked across at each other, then said, together:

'Well, it's happened—and there's nobody I would rather be with than you.'

Fortunately *Pisces III* did not appear to have suffered any damage in its fall. The radio still worked, so they were able to keep

At last! After a five-hour search, the mini-sub *Pisces V* locates her stricken sister ship, stranded 230 fathoms down on the sea bed.

in touch with *Vickers Voyager.* After he heard their report the mother-ship's skipper, Captain Leonard Edwards, gave one brief instruction:

'Lie down—shut up.'

The two trapped men prepared to follow his order to the letter. By keeping still and not talking, they would use the least possible amount of air. Although they had a good supply of this they realised there was certainly no sense in squandering it—or tempting fate, because there was no knowing how long they would be trapped on the sea floor.

Pisces III is winched from the sea bed by the rescue ship *John Cabot*– just in time.

On board *Vickers Voyager* Captain Edwards had already started organising the rescue. He ordered a marker buoy to be placed to show where *Pisces III* had gone down, and sent radio messages to other ships in the area and their own headquarters in England. By 6 pm that Wednesday another ship, *Sir Tristram,* had arrived to take over

He knew the score

Leading the *Pisces III* rescue operation was Commander Peter Messervy, general manager of Vickers Oceanic—a man who knew only too well just what it was like to be trapped in a submarine on the sea bed.

Three years earlier Commander Messervy had survived a similar accident. He was trapped with a companion in another *Pisces* vessel for nearly six hours, 100 fathoms (180 metres) down off British Columbia.

His *Pisces* had sunk because a vent plug—which had been removed during maintenance work—had not been replaced, and part of the sub was flooded.

Fortunately a Royal Canadian Navy mini-sub which was operating nearby came to the rescue. Within two hours a line had been attached to Commander Messervy's *Pisces*, and the sub was winched up.

watch at the scene of the accident, thus releasing *Vickers Voyager* to speed to Cork, 240 kilometres (150 miles) away, to collect rescue equipment.

Two other mini-submarines, *Pisces V* and *Pisces II,* were flown to Cork to help in the rescue, the first from Canada, the other from Tees-side in the north of England. By 10.30 on Thursday morning all the rescue equipment and the rescue team were on board *Vickers Voyager,* which was racing back to the disaster zone.

Meanwhile the weather had changed for the worse. A 40-knot (75 kph) gale had sprung up, and

by Thursday evening there was little that could be done to rescue the trapped men. Mallinson and Chapman had only about 60 hours' supply of air left, and nobody knew when the weather would improve. For more than 36 nerve-racking hours the operation was held up. Time was running out.

However, the two trapped men were doing everything they could to keep the odds stacked in their favour. Realising that the storm was delaying the rescue attempt, they saved their precious air supply by deliberately letting the amount of carbon

dioxide in it rise higher than the recommended safety level. As a result, carbon dioxide poisoning affected them, causing blinding headaches and spasms of pain in every limb. But the air lasted just that much longer.

What allowed the submariners enough air in the first place was an unexpected stroke of luck. The day before their undersea mission, Roger Mallinson was carrying out maintenance work aboard *Pisces III,* and decided to change the air tanks for two completely full ones. There was no real reason for him to do so, for the two tanks held up to 1,360 kilogrammes (3,000 lb) of air, and one of the tanks still had enough air in it for the eight-hour operation. As it happened, Mallinson's hunch paid off.

Their food supply could have been better. All the captives had was a cheese sandwich, half a

The ordeal is over with a thumbs-up signal from Roger Mallinson as the two rescued submariners speed to safety aboard an inflatable dinghy.

flask of coffee, and the normal emergency rations of glucose tablets and biscuits. They also found a sealed can which they hoarded until the moment *Pisces V* —after searching for them for almost seven hours—finally linked a line to the sunken sub. Then they ceremoniously broke open the can and drank a toast —in lemonade.

On the morning of Saturday, September 1, a US Navy CURV—a robot grappler—was lowered to the sea bed alongside the marooned sub. It thrust a specially-designed grappling-iron into *Pisces III*'s damaged after hatch. The iron locked into place, and *Pisces III* was gently winched back to the surface by the ship *John Cabot.*

Then, 76 hours after they plummetted helplessly to the bottom of the sea, Mallinson and Chapman thrust back the hatch and breathed fresh, salt-tanged air again. It was all the more welcome because they had only 90 minutes' supply left on board. They had come very close to complete disaster.

Instant design

Pisces III's rescue was all the more remarkable because of the grappling-iron which was used. It was designed by Vickers' technical manager, Harold Pass, especially for the operation.

Basically, it worked like an umbrella—and Pass designed it in less than 15 minutes. He said: 'Once I'd sketched it out, the technical department, working flat out, had completed one of the hooks in two hours. We didn't have anything like it, because we never thought it would be necessary.'

The US Navy CURV gently lowered the folded 'umbrella' in through the broken hatch. Then the weighted spokes opened out, preventing the grappling iron from pulling clear while the mini-sub was hauled to the surface. Without it *Pisces III* could not have been easily lifted.

TRAPPED UNDER AN AVALANCHE
The escape of Gerhard Freisegger

Struggling through thick snow, bowed before the freezing wind that swept across Austria's steep-sided Sattelalp, a group of workmen were making their way up the mountain towards the site of the new hydro-electric scheme at Heiligenblut. Suddenly they stopped, looked around . . . and listened. Was it the wind they had heard keening across the lonely mountains? Just as they were about to carry on, the sound came again. It was a muffled, human cry: 'Hilfe . . . Hilfe!' (Help!) Then a thin, bruised arm reached out of the snow a few yards away.

Rushing forward, the workmen dug the snow back and gently eased out Gerhard Freisegger, a man they had all thought was dead. He had made one of the most astounding escapes in the world. On that morning, February 2, 1951, the Austrian mechanic had survived, more dead than alive, after being buried for 13 days beneath an avalanche.

'A thin, bruised arm reached out of the snow . . .'

Gerhard and his colleague Siegfried Lindner were working on a hydro-electric scheme. They were based at a supply station halfway up the Sattelalp, collecting supplies from a cable car for Heiligenblut, a little village further up the mountain. On Saturday, January 21, Gerhard should have had the day off work. Instead he switched with a third man, who was married.

The weather was vicious. Strong winds blasted snow across the mountainside until late afternoon when they had to call a halt and return to the warmth of their hut. Once inside they stoked up

the fire and settled down for a comfortable evening, listening to the gale screaming outside. Just before Siegfried and Gerhard went to bed Winkelstation phoned through an avalanche warning. There seemed little to worry about, because Winkelstation was even higher up the mountain and more vulnerable to avalanches.

Shortly after two o'clock in the morning, Gerhard woke suddenly from sleep. The winds outside had increased in strength, almost seeming to rip off the strong roof from their cabin. Then, just when he was about to snuggle down even more beneath his blankets, he heard a thunderous roar outside. Something came crashing down on the cabin and everything collapsed around him. The avalanche had struck.

In total darkness, Gerhard struggled to free himself from the dead weight, which pinned him to his bunk. Snow and debris were all about him, pinning down both legs and his left side. Only his head and right arm were still free, because one of the beams from the roof had fallen over him, keeping the snow at bay. Literally tons and tons of snow had hurtled down on the cabin. Faintly, Gerhard could hear Sieg-

fried calling for help, but he was unable to move. Gerhard called back: 'Keep calm, old friend, keep calm. We'll soon be rescued.' A few hours later, Siegfried's voice died away and Gerhard guessed that his friend was dead.

Fortunately, the one thing Gerhard had dreaded—the cold —was kept at bay by the blankets and bedclothes wrapped around him. So he willed himself not to panic, but to lie back and relax in the awful silent darkness pressing down all around him, and wait for the rescue team that he knew would arrive in the morning.

Gerhard woke with a start some hours later. Faintly, through the heavily-packed snow surrounding him he could hear voices. The rescue party had arrived. He could hear them probing through the snow, trying to locate the cabin. It must be morning. Obviously, the rescue team were having trouble in finding the cabin. Gerhard heard the sound of their voices, the thump of their probes through the snow, coming and going.

Gerhard began to shout for help. Then he remembered that many people who had survived avalanches had remarked on the way in which the snow stifled their cries, while letting them hear the voices outside. So he began clawing away at the snow above him with his free hand. Certainly, his rescuers did not give up their search easily. Their determination to locate the cabin was matched only by Gerhard's determination to escape from his

trap. It was sheer will-power that goaded him on to scrape away at the surrounding snow with one hand, clawing away a little at a time. His only source of nourishment was the hard-packed snow, abundant but inadequate. Yet it meant all the difference between survival and failure.

It was almost seven days before Gerhard Freisegger had dug away enough snow to free his legs, and then his other arm. Then he discovered among the debris a broken piece of timber which helped his progress. Because of the lack of food over so many days Gerhard became weaker and weaker, but he dug on and forever upwards towards the sound of the rescue party. In continual darkness time had lost all meaning for Gerhard, until he woke up one day and saw a faint, grey, glow of daylight at the end of the tunnel which he had been so doggedly scraping. It seemed like an eternity before his length of timber finally broke through the surface and freezing fresh air rushed towards him.

By the time Gerhard

crawled towards the hole it was growing dark. As he fell asleep again, the thought crossed his mind that after such an effort he could well freeze to death before morning. Miraculously, he survived the night. But he was numb with cold, aching with hunger and so weak that he felt more dead than alive as he peered out into the snow-covered landscape beyond his tunnel.

Gerhard Freisegger knew that he could never expect to survive another day in his weakened condition in the Alpine cold. And then he heard the sound of those workmen trudging towards him along the slopes of the Sattelalp.

'Literally tons and tons of snow had hurtled down on the cabin.'

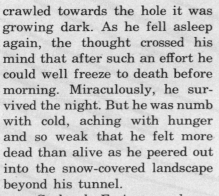

Buried alive

That is a good morning's hunting, thought Evert Stenmark as he put the four ptarmigan he had snared into his knapsack. Then suddenly the snow beneath his feet began to move. An avalanche was beginning. Faster and faster it went, sweeping him off his feet and hurling him down the hillside.

Suddenly it stopped, and all was quiet. But the 25-year-old Swede was buried alive, and no matter how much he struggled he could not find any way out of his icy tomb. Thinking quickly, he burrowed about like a mole to make a small chamber for his body before the snow froze hard again.

Evert was well dressed for the cold winter weather of that January Friday in 1955. Under his knee-high boots he wore double socks, and he had also lined the boots with reeds—what the Lapps call 'shoe hay'.

The young hunter knew a rescue party would soon be out searching for him. It was a question of waiting—and wait he did, living on snow and raw ptarmigan meat.

Evert found a long stick buried with him. Every day he pushed it through the snow overhead, to allow air to enter his icy prison. In his pockets he found some snare wire, and two bright red theatre tickets. He wired the tickets on to the end of the stick. And it was these tickets which Evert's brother Kjell spotted on the eighth day of the rescue hunt. Evert was saved.

OVER NIAGARA
10~year~old boy's escape

As he stared in horror through the thick cloud of spray at the bottom of Horseshoe Falls, Captain Clifford Keech could hardly believe his eyes. Bobbing along the Niagara River towards his crowded passenger steamer, *The Maid of the Mist*, was a small terrified boy wearing a bright orange lifejacket. While the boy was swept closer to the launch's whirling propellers Captain Keech quickly ordered his engines into reverse, so that the launch pulled back and the boy drifted safely past on the current.

The boy was seven-year-old Roger Woodward and on that Saturday morning, July 9, 1960, he had survived a terrifying ordeal. He had been swept over Niagara Falls. Just a few hours earlier neither Roger nor his 13-year-old sister Deanne could have dreamed that they were both to have narrow escapes from death. They were overjoyed when their father's friend Jim Honeycutt offered to take them for a cruise along the Niagara River, above the Falls, in his motor-launch. The children were even more excited when Honeycutt promised that they would be able to glimpse the famous waterfalls from above during their river trip.

Certainly, there did not appear to be anything to worry about, because Jim Honeycutt was an experienced boatman, whose launch was equipped with a 7½-horsepower outboard engine. And, very sensibly, the moment the children climbed into the launch Honeycutt insisted that

'A small, terrified boy wearing a bright orange lifejacket...'

they strapped on the two lifejackets which were on board. There was no jacket left for him. Soon the launch was cruising along the fast-flowing river, heading downstream towards the distant sound of the Falls. Then the launch reached the Remedial Works Control Dam, which stretches halfway across the river from the

'Every time the lifebelt was swept away from him by the waves and current.'

The awesome might of the American Falls at Niagara, dwarfing *The Maid of the Mist* on the left.

Canadian side. Everybody who visits Niagara Falls is shown the dam by tourist guides, who explain that it 'marks the point of no return' for boats: anybody sailing past the dam is swept relentlessly over the Falls. Whether Jim Honeycutt did not realise that, or whether he was too absorbed in watching the children enjoying themselves, nobody will ever know. The two factors that led to the disaster were that the launch had gone past the point of no return—and as Jim Honeycutt steered the launch round to go back upstream the propeller shaft snapped off.

Jim Honeycutt grabbed two oars and struggled to row the launch out of danger, but he was too late. The powerful current seized the boat and carried it into the racing rapids, which sent it bucking and twisting towards the very brink of the Niagara Falls. Screaming, the children clung to the sides of the boat. Then it somersaulted into the air and sent all three into the water.

Jim Hayes, a truck driver from New Jersey, had been taking photographs of the Falls from the guard rail at Terrapin Point on Goat Island when he spotted the upturned launch coming downstream towards him with Deanne clinging to it. Wedging one foot inside the railings, Hayes stretched himself out over the rapids, then reached out his hand to Deanne. She strained up and seized his thumb. Another tourist, John Quattrochi, also climbed over the guard railings and reached out for Deanne's other hand. Then inch by inch the two men dragged the terrified girl from the brink of death. Deanne sobbed at them to try and save her brother, too. But by then there was no sign of Roger or Jim Honeycutt. Both had been swept over the Falls.

Down below the Horseshoe Falls, Captain Keech had deliberately reversed *The Maid of the Mist* away from Roger, to avoid the risk of the boy being swept into the screws. Then, circling his vessel around, he approached Roger from upstream.

Two crewmen crouched in the bows of the steamer with a lifebelt attached to a rope, which they threw several times to Roger, but every time it was swept away from him by the waves and swift current. Finally it was thrown so close that it almost knocked Roger out, but he seized it and was carefully pulled on board.

Back at the children's home at Sunny Acres, Niagara, their parents had no idea that anything had happened until a police car stopped outside their front door just before lunch. For the first time the Woodwards heard the news that their son had been swept over the Falls and that their friend Jim Honeycutt was missing.

'We'll probably recover Jim's body by about Wednesday,' remarked one of the policemen. He was correct: four days later Niagara Falls gave up the body, which surfaced close to the boat that had saved Roger's life.

Later, experts from the Niagara Parks Commission explained Roger Woodward's miraculous escape. The main reason was that his slight weight, with help from the lifejacket, had shot him into the foam and prevented him being sucked down into the current.

'He rode Niagara Falls like a cowboy on a bucking bronco,' was the official explanation. 'If he had been dragged down by the current he would never have survived.'

BATTLE WITH THE NORTH SEA

Resistance heroes escape

Oluf Olsen

Norway in the summer of 1940 was not a pleasant place to be. This peaceful northern country, which had been keeping out of the turmoil of World War II then raging in Europe, suddenly found itself occupied by German troops. Adolf Hitler, the German Nazi leader, needed Norway's natural resources of iron for his war effort, so he invaded the country without warning on April 9, 1940. The Norwegians were powerless to resist—openly. But many men and women joined underground resistance movements, sabotaging German bases and lines of communication, and also spying on behalf of Britain, Germany's chief enemy and Norway's ally.

Among the resistance workers were two young men, Kaare Moe and Oluf Olsen. Because they were untrained, they had many narrow escapes from arrest, and they decided their best move would be to go to Britain, where they could join the Free Norwegian Air Force and learn the technique of war properly. The only way to do this was to buy a boat and sail across the North Sea. The Germans were already in control of all harbours, and allowed the sale of boats only on permit, but Kaare and Oluf managed, with much difficulty, to find a vessel. She was small—only 5.5 metres (18 feet) long, and she leaked like a sieve. The two young men persuaded a friendly boat-builder to mend her. Then they obtained, through the resistance movement, some forged papers which allowed them to sail

up and down the coast. Their excuse was that they were commercial travellers, and could not get petrol for their car. Optimistically, they named their boat *Haabet*—'Hope'—and provisioned her with 27 litres (6 gallons) of drinking water and whatever food they could find.

The two men set out from Oslo on September 2, sailing slowly along the coast through the Skagerrak, the channel between Norway and Denmark. At their first port of call they had a real scare: the police demanded to see their papers, as they were looking for two escaped criminals. Fortunately the descriptions of the wanted men did not match those of Kaare and Oluf.

A few days later they slipped out to sea under cover of darkness—but while they were still within sight of the shore a German destroyer ordered them back to port. But they had taken the precaution of having fishing permits, and pleaded that they had been blown off course. The Germans were satisfied—and Kaare and Oluf breathed a sigh of relief. After a few more days in harbour, they set out once more: but this time there were three of them. A young bank clerk named Rolf Gabrielson had persuaded them to let him come too. Once more storms forced them back, but on September 14 luck was with them, and a favourable wind sent them scudding towards Britain—and freedom.

Almost at once two German air force planes roared overhead,

and fired warning shots. However, bad weather soon stopped the attack from the air. Hour after hour the three men pumped water out of the leaky old boat. At last another plane spotted them, a British one this time. It exchanged signals by lamp, and promised to send a rescue craft. They were very close to the coast of Scotland.

Before they could celebrate, a storm came up suddenly from the west. Winds lashed them and huge waves pounded the boat. The mainsail split and vanished, the tiller was smashed, the pump broke down, and more leaks appeared. Courageously the three men fought to keep their craft afloat, although at one stage the boat was three-quarters full of water. They bailed non-stop, using a bucket and a hat. When the storm died down land was in sight: they had been blown right back across the North Sea almost to the coast of Denmark.

Once again good luck followed bad: the wind changed, and a strong breeze sent them towards the south-east of England. It also took them through a minefield, and more than once their hearts were in their mouths as the little craft sailed perilously close to these floating explosives. Day followed weary day, but at last the three men's perseverance was rewarded: they were sighted by another British plane, and a couple of hours later they were hailed by a British destroyer. They were just 32 kilometres (20 miles) off the mouth of the River Thames. Soon after a second war-ship came up, took the young Norwegians aboard and hoisted their gallant boat on deck. Almost at once a heavy sea washed her away, but by then Kaare, Oluf and Rolf were content: after fifteen days they had escaped both from the Germans and from the fury of the North Sea.

'Day followed weary day . . . until they were sighted by another British plane.'

Back into danger

The adventures of Oluf Olsen and his friends did not end with their safe arrival in England. They went to Canada to be trained as pilots, and there Kaare Moe was killed in a crash.

Oluf and Rolf Gabrielson returned to England, and active service with the Royal Air Force. Then in 1943 Oluf was parachuted into Norway, to act as a secret service agent with the Resistance Movement. He landed in a tree and dislocated his knee—but managed to put the joint back himself and went on to organise an efficient spy network and radio links with England. After a series of hair-raising adventures, keeping barely one jump ahead of the Germans, Oluf finally escaped to neutral Sweden and returned to England.

After only four months he was asked to go back and continue the work, and on May 6, 1944, he floated down into a bilberry bush.

He spent the rest of the war, in his own words, 'skulking like a hunted beast', until May 8, 1945, when peace came.

LOST IN THE JUNGLE
Girl's escape from wrecked plane

It was the torrential rain splattering through the dense forest foliage that roused Juliane Koepcke slowly back to consciousness. Dazed and unable at first to focus her eyes, she heard thunder rumbling overhead, so loud that it almost drowned the croaking of frogs and the chirruping of insects. Moments later, the 16-year-old German schoolgirl looked around and realised that she was lying in the wreckage of an aeroplane. One shoe was missing and her foot was bleeding. Her head was badly bruised around one eye, she felt her collar-bone was broken. . . and there was no sign of any other survivor.

Incredibly, Juliane had lived through an air crash, but it was only to find herself alone, injured and defenceless, in the impenetrable Amazonian rain-forests of Peru. Countless people have perished in similar circumstances, but this slender teenager was to make a remarkably determined escape from the wilderness. For she trekked 25 kilometres (15½ miles) through trackless jungle, during which she was constantly in peril from snakes, alligators, poisonous spiders and stingrays, as well as the ferocious flesh-eating piranha fish in the rivers.

Juliane's dramatic story began just after 11 o'clock on the morning of Christmas Eve, 1971, when she and her mother, Dr Maria Koepcke, were among some 90 passengers and crew who boarded the Lockheed Electra aircraft at Lima, Peru's capital. They took off for an hour-long flight across the Andes Mountains to Pucallpa, in northern Peru, where Juliane's father, Dr. Hans Koepcke, was waiting to celebrate Christmas with his family.

Half-an-hour after take-off their plane flew over the majestic, snow-capped peaks straight into an electrical storm. Turbulence shook the plane so badly that hand-luggage spilled from the overhead racks, while the passengers struggled to fasten their seat belts. Juliane glanced through a porthole to see the starboard engine burst into flames. Passengers screamed as the storm

Juliane Koepcke: a photograph taken a few months after her ordeal in the tropical forest.

hurled the plane about in the sky. Juliane remembers her mother's last words: 'My God—this is the end.' The plane began to break up, and just before Juliane blacked out, she felt herself hurtling through the air, watching the tree-tops coming nearer and nearer. Then, mercifully, she lost consciousness before the plane hit the ground.

It was shortly after daybreak on Christmas Day when Juliane felt strong enough to crawl out from the debris. There was no sign of her mother. Fortunately, Juliane was no stranger to the South American forest and its dangers. Between 1967 and 1969 she had lived with her parents at a remote research station at Pucallpa and during those two years she had learned valuable lessons about survival. She knew that spiders, flies, mosquitoes and ants were more common than large animals such as jaguars —but spiders and insects could be just as dangerous as the jaguars. She knew also that her best hope of escape was to find a river and to

Left: Alligators were among the perils Juliane faced. Right: The Shebonya River, along which she travelled.

follow its course to safety, because in many places the rivers are the highways of the Amazonian rain forests.

Juliane realised that she would need food of some sort for her journey. There was plenty of fruit growing in the forest. Some of it looked temptingly delicious, but Juliane knew most was deadly poisonous. All that she could find in the aeroplane wreckage was a Christmas cake that had been spoiled by the rain, and a bag of candies.

Armed with a large stick to ward off snakes and carrying the bag of candies, Juliane set off through the jungle to search for a river. Her progress was slow, because she was still suffering from shock after the crash. She was weakened by her injuries and had only one shoe. It was also the rainy season, so time and time again she was forced to shelter from heavy rain. Late on Christmas Day, however, after many weary hours of pushing through dense undergrowth and clambering across fallen trees, Juliane discovered a shallow stream, which meandered lazily through the jungle. That stream became her lifeline to safety and she set out to follow it until it flowed into a larger river. No matter how hard it was to keep beside the stream, she pressed doggedly on. Never once did she stray from its bank, because she knew that once the stream was out of sight she might never find it again.

During the next few days Juliane lost track of time. Her dress was ripped to shreds, exposing her back, which became badly burned by the sun. The most persistent and irritating problem, though, was the flies and mosquitoes which plagued her. Juliane did not realise it at first, but every time a blow-fly stung her, it laid eggs beneath her skin. These eggs rapidly hatched out into maggots. Several times Juliane heard aeroplanes circling overhead close to the tree-tops. Once she spotted a helicopter through the branches of the trees. She shouted and waved her arms:

'Help! Help! Oh, please, help me—I'm down here.' But the pilots could neither see nor hear her. Eventually, they widened their search for the missing plane and survivors, leaving Juliane sobbing helplessly as the sounds of the engines died away.

It might have been the third day, or perhaps the fourth day, when Juliane discovered that her precious store of candies was gone. She was so worn out by her ordeal that she failed to notice the bag was torn and some of the candies had dropped through the hole. Now it took a great deal of will-power to keep herself from snatching up the luscious-looking berries she came across and cramming them into her mouth. Juliane's memories of that time became so confused that she recalls little of her day-to-day struggles. Yet she remembers being constantly terrified in case she trod on a snake, the fear of stepping on a poisonous thorn with her naked foot.

And she will never forget the torment caused by those blow-fly stings. For the wounds they caused became painful and infected, as the maggots grew to 12 millimetres (half an inch) long and began feeding on her flesh. Some of these wounds became so deep that she could push a finger inside, and her left arm became so swollen that she was afraid it would have to be amputated. She broke a ring into two pieces, so that when she rested she could scrape out some of the small parasites; but there were too many to deal with.

One of Juliane's greatest disappointments came when she finally stumbled out into a clearing on the banks of a wide river. It was the main course of the Shebonya River, but she knew from the completely fearless behaviour of the wild animals that there were no villages or houses nearby. The creatures had not learned to be afraid of humans. She had no choice but to follow the fast-flowing river for as long and as far as she could. Sometimes she walked, or

crawled, along the banks. Sometimes she swam, letting the current carry her along like a piece of driftwood. Juliane realised that her wounds could well attract a shoal of deadly piranha fish and that poisonous stingrays often lurked beneath the mud, but she would not give up.

Juliane had covered more than 20 kilometres (12 miles) of the Shebonya and had lost all track of time, when she saw a small boat moored to the river bank. There was also a track leading into the forest. A few metres along the track she discovered a small hut, inside which were an outboard motor and a can of petrol wrapped up in a large plastic sheet. But there was no sign of any people.

That night, wrapped up in the plastic sheet, with only her head exposed, Juliane Koepcke slept undisturbed by the swarms of mosquitoes and other insects for the first time since the plane crash. The next morning Juliane rested beside the boat to take stock of her situation. She could not bring herself to steal the boat and anyway she knew that she could not operate the engine. There was no point, either, in waiting there for the owners to return. They might be away for days—they might even have perished in the forest. Then, just when she was about to continue with her lone journey, Juliane heard movement behind her. Glancing round she saw three young men coming out of the forest.

For the first time in 10½ days she heard the sound of another human voice as one of the men exclaimed: 'Hey, who are you?' She was saved.

Juliane shows how she waded in the river to find her way through the forest. She knew that if she left the waterway she might never find her way back to civilisation and safety. She bravely went back to the jungle to show photographers how she managed to escape to civilisation.

THE WILY ADVENTURER

Casanova escapes from jail

A contemporary painting of Giacomo Casanova, made when he was a young man.

Giacomo Casanova was one of the greatest adventurers the world has ever seen. He was born in 1725, the son of an actor, and by his own efforts became notorious in 18th century European society. He was the friend of princes, nobles and philosophers; a confidence trickster of amazing ability; and above all a great lover.

Casanova was a Venetian. At that time Venice was more than a city: it was a small country, ruled by a doge (he was the chief magistrate of Venice) and a council. Casanova's many activities brought him into conflict several times with the government of Venice, and at last the authorities acted. On July 26, 1755, Casanova's lodging was invaded by Messer Grande, the chief of police, together with 40 archers. They dragged him off to the doge's palace, and there he was taken to a prison cell. The cells were in the attics of the palace, just under the leaded roof, and were known as 'The Leads'. Casanova's cell was only 1.5 metres (5 feet) high, stiflingly hot from the sunshine beating on the roof.

Nobody actually bothered to tell him why he was imprisoned, though the official records show that the charges were witchcraft and being 'an enemy to religion'. As the weeks went by Casanova, a tall, vigorous man with a resolute, ingenious mind, determined to escape. He was allowed to take exercise in another, larger room, where he found an iron bar and a slab of marble. Painfully he sharpened the bar on the stone, and began to bore a hole in the floor. Thirteen months after he entered prison he was ready to get away.

'He sharpened the bar ... and began to bore a hole.'

Then to his horror the head jailer came in one day with good news: he was to be moved to a much better, larger cell! Protesting, Casanova was moved to the new cell, his iron bar accompanying him hidden in a chair. The jailer soon found the hole Casanova had made, but the wily adventurer shut his mouth by telling him that if he was denounced he would say the jailer helped him.

Undaunted, Casanova now conspired with a prisoner in the next cell, Father Marin Balbi, a priest. They communicated by exchanging books, and writing messages in them. Balbi cut a hole in the ceiling of his cell, which led into a small attic over both compartments. He covered

a prison. There Casanova found a dormer window and broke it open. He lowered Balbi through it on the rope—to find that the window was 7.5 metres (25 feet) above the floor. There was nothing he could tie the rope to so that he could slide down himself. Casanova set off to explore the palace roof more thoroughly, and found a ladder left there by builders. At great danger he lowered the ladder through the dormer window— nearly falling off the roof in the process.

Safely in the huge room below, Casanova took a short sleep. Then, roused by the agitated Balbi, he broke open a door, and the two men set about finding their way out of the palace,

'At great danger he lowered the ladder through the window, nearly falling off.'

'The two men spent several hours tearing up sheets ... to make a rope.'

the hole with a picture of a saint —indeed, he plastered all the walls of his cell with such pictures as camouflage.

One night Balbi broke through the ceiling of Casanova's cell, and the two men spent several hours tearing up sheets and blankets to make a rope. Each had a cell-mate, whom they terrified into helping them. With his iron bar Casanova cut a hole in the roof of the attic, forced back the sheet of lead over it—and looked out at the Moon.

Casanova and Balbi climbed out on to the roof, 27 metres (90 feet) above ground. They decided to shuffle their way along the rooftop until they came to a part of the palace that was not used as

through a maze of rooms and corridors. They had to force several more doors, until finally they came to one they could not break. Luckily, somebody saw Casanova through the window of the room they were in, and the doorkeeper came to find out who had been shut in. As he gaped at the sight of two men where he did not expect to see anyone, the two escaping prisoners boldly walked past him, downstairs and out of the palace. At the nearby canal they hired a gondola—the taxi of Venice—and were borne swiftly away to freedom.

Even then it was a near thing. After the two men parted Casanova, weary and bedraggled, called at a house for help. He was

given food and a bed, and then went on his way. It was the house of a police chief who was away —leading the search for Casanova and Balbi.

Casanova lived to have many more adventures, finally dying in Bohemia at the age of 73.

'At the nearby canal they hired a gondola.'

FLIGHT FROM TIBET

The escape of the Dalai Lama

The Dalai Lama (right) during his daring escape from Tibet.

Swirling all around Lhasa, Tibet's holy city, was one of the fiercest sandstorms in living memory. It blotted out the afternoon sun, forcing thousands of Buddhist pilgrims to crouch down on the ground and cover themselves with their long robes. The Chinese troops surrounding the Nor-bu-gling-ka Summer Palace huddled down into their overcoats too, unable to see more than a few metres in any direction.

Yet to the Buddhist monks and Tibetan government officials attending a meeting with the Dalai Lama inside the palace that sudden sandstorm on March 15, 1959, was a magnificent omen. It provided the ideal opportunity for the Dalai Lama—their god-king—to make his escape from the Chinese soldiers who had invaded his country and enslaved his subjects. To millions of devout Tibetans, the Dalai Lama was not simply a 24-year-old monarch, but the reincarnation of the first Dalai Lama.

The Dalai Lama and his advisers had submitted meekly when the Chinese forces invaded their country back in 1951 because they realised that a war would be disastrous. Unfortunately, that peaceful attitude did not stop their conquerors from taking over the land and farms or from claiming heavy taxes which were forcing Buddhist monasteries to close. Then the young Khams-pa tribal leader Chief Andrutschang launched a guerrilla offensive against the Chinese, and, within months, he was leading an army of 12,000 rebels.

The guerrilla operations became so successful that the Chinese planned to remove the Dalai Lama from the country, hoping that without his presence and influence the guerrillas might lose heart. The Chinese governor of Tibet, General Tan Kuan-san, tried to invite the Dalai Lama to visit Peking, but the high lamas (priests) and Tibetan government ministers so successfully surrounded their god-king that no Chinese official was able to approach him with the formal invitation.

The Tibetans had been warned about the Chinese plans. They feared for the Dalai Lama's life once he left their protection. Then one of the Tibetan monks, who had become friendly with the Chinese, invited the Dalai Lama to attend a concert at the Chinese headquarters and added that he was expected to attend with only two or three unarmed attendants. The Dalai Lama politely accepted the invitation, but when his advisers heard about it they became angry, and started urging the god-king to escape to India.

The Dalai Lama was a determined young man with a strong sense of duty, who was not prepared to flee from Tibet merely to save his own life. First, he had to be convinced that he could do more to help his people from exile than he could by staying in Tibet, or even in China. For several days he postponed the visit to the Chinese headquarters and then he began planning his escape.

Finally General Tan Kuan-san lost patience because of the constant delays, and ordered his artillery to fire several warning shells into the Nor-bu-gling-ka Palace gardens to flush out the Dalai Lama. At 12 o'clock on March 15 two shells exploded in the palace grounds. Although

they did little damage, the Dalai Lama at last agreed to escape as soon as darkness fell. A few moments later the monster sandstorm sprang up, and it was regarded by the high lamas as 'a divine act of God'. The crack Tensing Khams-pa cavalry regiment was put on the alert to cover the Dalai Lama's flight. The cavalrymen were placed in small groups between the palace and the River Gyi-chu ('Happy River'), in strategic positions, and the main force prepared to pretend that the Dalai Lama's party had fled to the north. Thousands of Buddhist pilgrims had arrived in Lhasa that week to pay their respects to their leader during a religious festival. While they sheltered beneath their robes during the storm, not one recognised his Dalai Lama as he stole from the palace accompanied by two courtiers, all disguised as peasants. Nearly 90 other people, officials and members of the Dalai Lama's family, passed stealthily

in small groups unnoticed through the sandstorm. Within two hours they had all crossed the river and were riding south through the storm towards the distant Himalayas.

By midnight the escape party had started the arduous ride up into the mountains towards the hazardous Chela Pass, 4,800 metres (16,000 feet) up in the Himalayas: a dangerous, precipitous, sand-strewn track, which led to territory held by the Khams-pas. After riding all night they abandoned their horses and walked down into the valley of the Brahmaputra river, where the Tensing Khams-pa regiment had re-grouped to meet them and escort them to India.

Four hundred hand-picked members of the Khams-pa Khelenpa 'suicide squad' formed a rearguard, vowing to fight to the death before allowing the Chinese anywhere near their beloved Dalai Lama. Fortunately they did not have to fire as much

as a single shot, because the escape had been so skilfully handled that it was 65 hours before the Chinese discovered that he had slipped away from them.

For the next four weeks the Dalai Lama's party disappeared from sight. Travelling on foot and horseback across little-known mountain tracks, often by night to avoid being spotted from the air, they arrived safely in northern India, where the government allowed the Dalai Lama to live in exile peacefully.

When the Tibetans realised that their god-king had been forced to flee they rose in rebellion—a two-day slaughter in which 10,000 were killed. Since that time Tibet has been a province of China.

Astride a white pony the Dalai Lama, disguised as a peasant, rides doggedly up yet another slope on the long escape through the mountains, with his faithful escort guarding him.

OVER THE SEA TO SKYE

The escape of Bonnie Prince Charlie

Back in 1746 £30,000 was an enormous sum of money. At that time a farm worker and his family might earn less than £25 in a whole year. Yet that huge sum which was offered as a reward was not enough to buy off the loyalty of hundreds of Scots to Charles Edward Stuart, the man known to history as Bonnie Prince Charlie, or the Young Pretender.

Charles Edward Stuart, the man with the £30,000 price on his head, was the son of James Edward, himself the son of the deposed Stuart king James II. James Edward claimed the thrones of England and Scotland as James III, and in 1745 his son

Charles landed in Scotland to raise a rebellion in his support. Thousands of Jacobites (followers of James) rallied to him, and the prince's army reached Derby on its march towards London. But there were not enough supporters in England: Charles retreated, and on April 16, 1746, at Culloden near Inverness, the Jacobites were completely overcome. Charles, stunned by his defeat, allowed himself to be led from the battlefield by a handful of his supporters.

So complete was the defeat that only one course remained for Charles: to escape to France by ship. The Western Highlanders were the Scots most loyal to the

Above: A contemporary painting of Bonnie Prince Charlie. Below: The defeat at Culloden.

Jacobite cause, and so Charles determined to make for the west coast, to await a French ship. In fact two French privateers were off the coast within two weeks of the battle, and took off several fleeing Jacobites; but Charles failed to make contact with them.

For the fugitive prince there followed days of stumbling on foot over rugged mountain tracks, resting sometimes in comfortable houses, at others in the roughest

possible shelter. Charles thought he would be safer in the lonely islands off the coast than on the mainland, and on the night of April 26 eight loyal boatmen rowed Charles and five supporters through a violent storm to the island of Benbecula in the Outer Hebrides. They spent the next few weeks rowing from one island to another, sheltering in huts. During this time the prince spent his time hunting, fishing and trying his hand at camp-fire cookery.

By early June the British government had got wind of Charles's presence in the Hebrides, and the seas were alive with warships looking for him, while parties of soldiers combed the islands. At this moment Charles was introduced to a brave girl, Flora MacDonald, who was staying with friends on Ben-

'Betty Burke' and Flora step on board a small boat.

becula. Flora agreed to travel to the island of Skye to visit her mother, taking with her a maid-servant, Betty Burke. Flora obtained passports for herself and her maid to pass through the parties of hunting soldiers. 'Betty Burke' was Charles, disguised in women's clothes. On the night of June 28 they were rowed, in the words of the old song,

'Over the sea to Skye'

'For the fugitive prince there followed days in hiding.'

and once again experienced a violent storm. On Skye Flora led him to the house of friends, who were surprised to see Flora accompanied by 'an odd muckle hussy' as one of them described 'Betty Burke'. After 12 days Charles said goodbye to Flora and—clad once more as a man—set off on his wanderings again. A few days later he was rowed back to the mainland of Scotland, where it was easier to conceal him.

For the next few weeks Charles roamed the wild mountainous region, sheltering in huts, caves, and woods, always on the lookout for soldiers. Meanwhile the French, hearing of Charles's wanderings, had sent more ships to pick him up. Fortunately the British government had the idea he would try to escape from the east coast of Scotland, and so a rendezvous was finally arranged at Loch nan Uamh, on the west coast, where Charles had landed to start the rebellion 14 months earlier. In the early morning of September 20 Charles and more than 100 other Jacobites were taken on board two French ships, and before the dawn broke they had slipped away to sea—and to safety in France.

THE HUNDRED DAYS

Napoleon escapes from Elba

A short, stocky man with gleaming eyes paced rapidly up and down in the palace of his tiny island kingdom. From the man standing respectfully beside him he had just heard the news he was longing for. 'Fleury,' he said, suppressing his inward excitement, 'I could be in France in two days if the nation were to recall me. Do you think I ought to go back?'

Fleury de Chaboulon pursed his lips. 'Sire,' he said cautiously, 'you have become the object of the adulation and hopes of the army and the nation.'

The bright-eyed man paused. 'My mind is made up,' he said, firmly.

That decision was to lead to an escape which struck terror into millions of people, and cost thousands of lives. For the decisive mind was that of the Emperor Napoleon, in exile on the small Mediterranean island of Elba. The date was February 13, 1815.

As Emperor of the French, Napoleon had conquered and ruled most of Europe. He was one of the greatest generals of the day, and his magnetic personality gave him many devoted followers. However, the peoples he had conquered were far from friendly towards him, and in 1814, after years of warfare, they combined to defeat him. On May 4, 1814, the man who had controlled the destinies of millions was exiled to Elba, where he was allowed to keep his title of Emperor, and have a court just like he did in the great days of his glory. The lands he conquered were freed from his rule, and France itself was governed by King Louis XVIII, a member of the Bourbon family which used to reign in France until the French Revolution began 25 years earlier.

However, Napoleon was far from finished. He was only 45 years old, very healthy and at the height of his powers. And the news Fleury de Chaboulon brought him was that the French people were unhappy under Louis's rule, and indeed some of them were conspiring to overthrow the king.

So, the question remained, how was Napoleon to escape? Although he was fully in control of Elba, he was constantly watched. The British had a small warship, the *Partridge*, patrolling the sea around the island, and a commissioner, or diplomatic representative, Sir Neil Campbell, lived on Elba. Here, luck played into the Emperor's hands. Three days later Campbell sailed aboard the *Partridge* to Italy for a few days. The warship returned to patrol Elba, but Napoleon's plans were now well advanced. He had his own small ship, the brig *L'Inconstant*, painted in the same colours as an English warship, and

Exile on Elba: the Emperor gazes out to sea.

he assembled his tiny army. News of his plans leaked out, and reached Campbell, but it was too late. On the night of February 26, as the *Partridge* picked Campbell up to bring him back to Elba, Napoleon embarked with 1,050 officers and men. To carry his force he had six smaller vessels as well as *L'Inconstant*.

Seven ships sailing together might arouse suspicion if anyone saw them, so the little fleet scattered, with a rendezvous at the Golfe de Juan, on the French Riviera not far from Nice. There was only one anxious moment,

Left: Napoleon at the moment of his landing in France (from an old woodcut). Below: the soldiers breaking ranks to rejoin their old leader (from a painting).

when Napoleon's ship encountered a French ship. There came a hail: 'How's Napoleon these days?' A quick word from the Emperor, and the captain of the brig shouted back 'Marvellously well!' The vessels passed; Napoleon breathed again. 'I shall reach Paris without firing a shot,' he told his anxious aides.

And so it proved. As Napoleon and his tiny army marched towards Grenoble, they encountered a royalist force. From one of its officers came the crisp order: 'There he is—fire on him!' Nobody moved for a moment, then Napoleon stepped forward, saying: 'Soldiers, if there is one among you who wishes to kill his Emperor, he can do so. Here I am.' With a loud cry of 'Long live the Emperor!' the royalist soldiers

broke ranks and ran cheering to join their old leader.

Two weeks later Napoleon was marching towards Paris at the head of 14,000 men, and on March 14 he was joined by one of his old marshals, Ney, who had previously been sent to stop him. Never has an escape provoked so much panic. Louis XVIII and his government fled from France to Ghent in Belgium. As the news spread people in other countries shuddered at the thought that 'the Corsican tyrant', as they called Napoleon, would again dominate Europe. At once steps were taken to deal with him. Austria, Britain, Prussia and Russia set to work to raise troops to crush the Emperor, whom they declared to be 'an outlaw'.

Two armies were raised

within a few weeks. One was a Prussian force of 120,000 men, commanded by Marshal Gebhard von Blücher. The other was a ragtail mixture of British, Dutch, Belgians and Germans, few of whom had any real experience of warfare, and many of whom had actually served under Napoleon only a year or two earlier. This force of 93,000 men was commanded by Britain's most experienced general, the Duke of Wellington, who described his army as 'infamous'. Now Napoleon had 124,000 men, all experienced. He also had the advantage that he could attack where he liked, while the opposing armies had to guard a long frontier. At first Napoleon seemed to be winning. He defeated the Prussians at the Battle of Ligny, and forced them to retreat, while another part of the French army fought an inconclusive battle with some of Wellington's troops at nearby Quatre Bras. Wellington retreated to a strong defensive position near the little village of Waterloo. There on June 18 he held off a series of massive French attacks. At dusk the Prussian army arrived to help, Napoleon was finally and soundly defeated, and he fled in dismay from the battlefield.

That was the end of the Escape from Elba. On June 22 Napoleon abdicated again, after a second reign so short that it has become known as 'The Hundred Days'. This time his opponents were taking no chances, and the Emperor spent his last few years on the lonely island of St. Helena in the South Atlantic. From that island there was to be no escape.

The Battle of Waterloo: French cavalry charging a Scottish regiment of infantry, which has formed into squares to resist the attack (painting by Félix Philippoteaux).

Napoleon's last home: Longwood House on the island of St. Helena. It was originally built to house cattle, and it was damp (from an old engraving).

ANTARCTIC EPIC

Expedition escapes from the ice

For eleven months the expedition ship *Endurance* had been gripped by ice in the Weddell Sea. Now, in November 1915, the brief Antarctic summer was coming again, and the ice was breaking up. But the vice-like grip of the ice had done its work. The *Endurance* had been crushed and holed, and as her crew watched from the safety of a nearby ice-floe, she slid beneath the icy waters of the southern seas.

'The expedition . . . was camped on a bleak, barren beach . . . and nobody knew where it was.'

The expedition's leader, Sir Ernest Shackleton, was undismayed. He and the *Endurance's* skipper, Commander F.A. Worsley, had prepared for the loss of the ship, and all 28 members of the party were huddled safely on a thick ice-floe, with their stores and three small but stout boats. For shelter they had flimsy tents, and they caught seals and penguins for food.

For five months the eleven scientists and seventeen sailors stayed on the ice-floe while it drifted 960 kilometres (600 miles) northwards. On April 9, 1916, the

Sir Ernest Shackleton

floe broke up beneath their feet, and hurriedly they launched their boats into a cold sea, surrounded by lumps of drifting ice and deadly killer whales. The nearest land was Elephant Island, a small, desolate lump of rock in the South Shetlands. After five

days of misery, sometimes aboard the boats, sometimes hauled out on ice-floes, they reached the island. They were safe—for a time.

The situation was still desperate. Winter was on them, they were camped on a bleak, barren beach and they had had to jettison part of their stores during their five-day ordeal. The worst part was that there was no hope of rescue, for nobody knew where they were. The *Endurance* should have been in the southern part of the Weddell Sea, 2,500 kilometres (1,600 miles) away—and that was where any search party would look for them. Having escaped to Elephant Island, they now had to escape from it. But how?

Shackleton, the bravest of men, had the answer. Twenty-eight men in three small boats could not possibly make it across the storm-tossed seas to the nearest inhabited place—but six men in the largest of the boats probably could. In any case, the nearest help was at Cape Horn or the Falkland Islands, and gales and swift-running seas would carry any boat away from both places. The only hope was to make north-eastwards to South Georgia, 1,400 kilometres (850 miles) away.

The boat selected for this epic journey was the *James Caird*, 6.85 metres (22 feet 6 inches) long and 1.8 metres (6 feet) wide. In this vessel, about the size of a large saloon car, Shackleton proposed to face the rigours of the southern winter. Although he had served in the Merchant Navy, he knew nothing about sailing small boats. Luckily Commander Worsley, a member of the party, was experienced, and one of the other four men was a former North Sea fisherman.

The others who made up the party worked to make the *James Caird* as seaworthy as possible, filling in the space between her fore and aft decks with sledge runners and box lids, covered with canvas. The men sewing the canvas had to thaw it out over an evil-smelling fire of seal blubber,

inch by inch, before they could get the needles into it. They also stitched sails for the boat.

On the morning of Easter Monday, April 24, 1916, the little party set out. They had with them food, water and fuel for a Primus stove to last them 30 days. For the first few hours they sailed through a mass of ice fragments, broken into fantastic shapes, looking like castles, towers, elephants, bears and a host of other creatures. By nightfall Elephant Island was just a smudge on the horizon, and all the ice had been left behind, too. Later they were to long for a lump of ice, which is fresh water, to give them something to drink.

Gradually the six men settled into a routine. Three kept watch and steered the boat for four hours at a time while the other three tried to sleep in the space under the deck, huddled in damp sleeping bags. The 'beds' were boxes containing stores. As the boat rose and fell with the waves the sleepers were bounced up and down till they were sore all over. So much water came into the boat from the seas breaking over her that she had to be pumped out every two hours.

What kept them going was regular hot meals. Two men sat in the largest part of the 'cabin', their backs to the sides of the boat, with the Primus stove jammed between their feet. In it the cook, Tom Crean, cooked 'hoosh', a mixture of lard, oatmeal, beef and vegetable protein, salt and sugar. This was supplied in the form of bricks, and when Tom boiled it in water it made a delicious, thick soup. With it the crew ate biscuits and lumps of sugar. Shackleton also insisted that hot milk, made with milk powder, was served every four hours when the watches changed.

After fourteen days came the cheerful cry: 'Land ho!' Worsley's navigation, in spite of all the difficulties, had brought them to South Georgia. The coast was desolate and forbidding, and soon it was out of reach. For a gale sprang up and quickly reached

'Three men kept watch and steered . . . while the other three tried to sleep.'

hurricane force. For hours the little boat hovered, clear of the shore, until the gale itself took a hand and drove it straight towards the island. For nine hours the six weary men fought to keep their little craft clear, until at last they were safe; still in the open sea though in sight of the rocks and cliffs of South Georgia. The storm had been so fierce that a 500-ton steamer bound for South Georgia from Argentina sank with all hands.

The next morning Shackleton and his men tried to find a landing spot, but the wind was blowing off shore. All day they struggled, racked by thirst, for

down a bit, then up again. Finally the three men halted on the edge of a steep slope. There was fog behind them, darkness ahead.

Was the slope safe to go down? 'We'll try it' said Shackleton. Holding on to each other, the three men set off to slide down on their bottoms. It was the most frightening part of the whole trip, but in about three minutes they came to rest, having covered about 1.6 kilometres (1 mile) and descended half the distance they had so painfully climbed. So the trip went on, hour after hour of climbing, descending, crossing ice slopes and continually checking their directions with a tiny pocket compass. From time to time they stopped to eat.

At last, after 36 hours of almost non-stop walking, three ragged, filthy men, with long hair and beards matted with soot and blubber, stumbled up to the Norwegian whaling station and asked for Captain Sorlee, the man in charge and an old friend of both Shackleton and Worsley. Sorlee did not recognise them . . .

Twelve hours later a steam whaler took Worsley back to fetch the other two men from the far side of the island. But it took 100 days and four attempts aboard rescue vessels to reach Elephant Island and bring the rest of Shackleton's expedition back.

their water was all gone. At last, just as darkness was falling, they beached the boat in a tiny cove. There was a stream with fresh water . . .

The men landed the stores and tried to haul the boat up the beach, but could not manage it. After a few hours sleep, while one man stood watch, they all had to work hard to save the boat from being swept away. It took them all the next day to make her safe.

Now came the problem. The South Georgia whaling station, where there was help, lay on the far side of the island. Two of the men were very weak—in fact, Shackleton said later that if they

had spent another night in the boat they would have died. Even after a few days' rest, with plenty of food—they killed a sea-elephant and some albatross chicks the size of turkeys—it was obvious that they could not sail the boat around the island. Neither the boat nor its crew was in a fit state to make the trip.

There was nothing for it but a slog overland, with a mountain pass 1,200 metres (4,000 feet) to cross. Shackleton, Worsley and Tom Crean, who were still fairly fit, set out on this stage of their journey on May 19. There followed a nightmare of climbing, cutting steps in the ice, going

Back to the war

Within weeks of the rescue all the members of the expedition were back in Europe and taking part in the fighting of World War I. Six months later Timothy Macarty, a cheerful Irishman who was the life and soul of Shackleton's boat journey, died when his ship went down. Shackleton and the others survived. In 1921 Shackleton set off on another Antarctic expedition, but in January 1922 he died suddenly in South Georgia, where he is buried.

LEOPARD BOY

South African lad's escape

Nigel Bonnett

The leopardess, snarling and spitting with fury, hurled itself repeatedly around its cage. Suddenly the doors burst open and the killer cat sprang free. Almost in the same swift movement it launched itself at the game warden crouching nearby. Then man and leopard were rolling across the ground in a grim life-or-death struggle.

The slender figure of a 16-year-old boy in a white shirt darted from a parked truck and hurled himself at the leopard. He was Nigel Bonnett, the game warden's son, and he plucked the leopard from his father with his bare hands. The animal swung round lithely on Nigel, its claws savaging his face and shoulders and its fangs seeking out a death grip on the boy's throat. What had started out as a pleasant day's outing in Nairobi National Park had turned into a nightmare.

Nigel's father, Harry Bonnett, was working in Kenya as an engineer and had also been appointed an honorary game warden for the national park. One Saturday morning in 1966 the Game Department telephoned him at home, asking if he could collect a killer female leopard and release it somewhere in the vast game reserve in the national park. To Nigel's delight, his father agreed and invited some friends to come with them on the trip to the game reserve.

Nigel and his father led the way in their truck. The caged leopard was in a trailer behind it, stout sacking covering its cage. Two other cars followed behind. Driving one was Elizabeth Giles, an English girl working in Kenya, with her parents. In the third car was another honorary game warden, Mr Ellis Monk, with his wife and children, and Mr Alexander Ross.

After several hours Harry Bonnett turned off at a remote corner of the game reserve and slowed to a stop. The two other vehicles halted on either side of the trailer, cameras ready, with those inside waiting to observe and photograph the beautiful leopardess as it made its graceful run to freedom.

Nigel watched his father uncovering the cage in the trailer and noticed how restless the leopard had become. Yet there was no inkling of danger. The release was something that Harry Bonnett had carried out many times in the past. All he had to do was unlock the cage doors, fix up a draw wire, which when pulled would slide the cage doors apart, and return to the safety of the truck to operate the mechanism.

Unfortunately the draw wire jammed, and the cage doors remained shut. Cautiously Harry Bonnett stepped from his truck, holding the door open with one hand, while he reached round the cage to pull the cage doors apart with his other hand. It was a long stretch. Just as his fingers reached out the leopard struck angrily through the bars. It missed his arm, but one razor-sharp claw hooked itself round his watch strap. Neither Harry Bonnett nor the leopardess could break free. So he released the truck door to use his other hand to loosen the watch strap. The truck door slammed shut. Harry Bonnett freed his wrist from the

'A 16-year-old boy in a white shirt . . . hurled himself on the leopard.'

enraged leopard—and that was when it came bounding through the cage doors.

Everything happened so quickly that none of the people in the other cars had time to move before Nigel threw himself into the fight. Only seconds had passed since the attack, but Nigel's own attack on the leopard sparked off action among the others. Shouting and screaming, they tried to frighten the leopard away. Then Elizabeth Giles started her car engine. Revving noisily, she drove slowly towards the leopard. It paused, snarling at the car, and then bounded off to disappear into the scrub.

Nigel and his father received urgent hospital treatment in Nairobi after their escape. There was no doubt that Nigel had saved his father's life, and his courage won him the Royal Humane Society's Silver Medal for his action.

The smallest park

Nairobi National Park is the smallest of Kenya's five nature reserves, but it is popular because it is very close to Nairobi, the country's capital. Children go by bus on guided tours round the park, supervised by wardens, to learn how valuable and important the wildlife of their country is.

But neither the children nor any other members of the public are allowed to get out of their vehicles in the reserve.

The park has an animal hospital and orphanage, where sick animals are nursed and young ones which have lost their parents can be cared for.

THE WOODEN HORSE

World War II escape drama

Oliver Philpot

Displayed in London's Imperial War Museum is one of the strangest relics from any war. It is the replica of a crudely-made wooden vaulting horse, the sort that can be seen in almost any school gymnasium. What is so special about this vaulting horse is that the original was instrumental in helping three British officers to make one of World War II's most daring escapes from a prisoner-of-war camp in Nazi Germany.

In the spring of 1943 Eric Williams and Michael Codner were just two of the hundreds of officers imprisoned in Stalag Luft III, in Silesia. They were also just two of the hundreds of officers who spent their time devising ways in which they could escape.

It was Michael Codner who first hit upon the idea of turning a vaulting horse into a 'Trojan Horse' as the cover for an escape tunnel. The plan was beautifully simple, as most of the best escape plans were. The horse was made so that one man could hide inside it. While it was in use he could dig away at the ground underneath it.

At the same time the plan was ambitious—for Williams and Codner had to dig, through sandy soil, a tunnel stretching from beneath the horse more than 37 metres (120 feet) to reach outside the perimeter fence of the camp. The only tool they had for this task was an ordinary bricklayer's trowel. But they had something much more valuable: unlimited determination to succeed.

When it was finished the vaulting horse stood 1.4 metres (4 feet 6 inches) high, with a base measuring 1.5 metres by 0.9 metres (5 feet by 3 feet). Four slots were cut in the sides, so that strong poles could be pushed through, allowing four men to carry the horse. Then a team of other prisoners was recruited to use the horse for regular vaulting sessions. The vaulters wore shorts, made by cutting the legs off their trousers. The legs were turned into bags for carrying the excavated sand away.

For the first week the plan was just to get the German guards used to the sight of the vaulting team in action. No work was done at all on the tunnel. There had been so many escape attempts that the Germans were suspicious of anything out of the ordinary, and it was essential to allay those suspicions.

During that first week, too, the guards had every opportunity to examine the wooden horse inside as well as outside. One vaulter was carefully chosen to play the 'clumsy guy' who from time to time knocked the horse over on its side.

Then the tunnel was started. Every day the horse was carried out from its storage place in the canteen, with either Eric Williams or Michael Codner hidden inside it. Hooks were screwed inside the horse, to which twelve of the trouser-leg bags were slung, carrying back the sand which had been dug out. The sand was scattered around the camp afterwards; some was hidden under the huts, some was scattered where it would not show, some was dug into the tomato patches outside the huts.

The sand, which was often

'A team of prisoners . . . used the wooden horse for regular vaulting sessions.'

wet, gave added weight to the horse. To make certain that the four men carrying it to and from the camp compound each day could cope with the weight, the man digging the tunnel could lengthen it by no more than 300 millimetres (1 foot) at a time.

It took more than a week to dig out the 1.5 metre (5 feet) deep entrance shaft and shore up its sides with wood. The shaft was concealed with a trapdoor, covered with a deep layer of sandbags and a top layer of loose soil so the guards could not locate it.

Two sandpits were dug in the compound, one at the top of the horse and the other at the side. The guards were led to believe these pits were to cushion the fall of the vaulters as they landed. In reality they were to enable the carriers to place the horse in exactly the same position each day, so that the diggers could locate the tunnel entrance.

The first short stretch of the tunnel had to be shored up with wood, too, because the vaulters were landing directly on top of it. After that the tunnel ran unsup-

ported. It was so narrow that only one man could work there at a time. He had to slither in like a snake, arms stretched in front of him, clutching the trowel in one hand and an empty sack in the other. He worked in complete darkness, with very little air, the sand seeping into his ears, eyes, nose and mouth, his muscles cramped by the angle at which he was digging.

The work was slow and dangerous. By the end of the first two months the tunnel was only 12 metres (40 feet) long, and Eric Williams and Michael Codner were both completely exhausted. The longer the tunnel became, the worse the air supply got, and the more time they had to spend beneath the ground. The lack of air was a serious problem, but they did not dare to push air holes to the surface because the Germans' guard dogs would soon sniff them out.

One day the whole escape plan was almost discovered. Michael Codner was burrowing away beneath the compound when the roof collapsed. The vaulters suddenly spotted a deep hole appearing in the ground. Quickly one of the team pretended to trip, throwing himself across the hole. While he lay there, feigning injury, he scooped sand into the hole, saving the day.

The only person who could save Michael Codner, completely buried by the subsidence, was himself. Slowly he scraped away the sand that covered him and shored up the sides of the tunnel again. By the time he had finished, Michael was so exhausted and shocked by his experience that he could scarcely drag himself and the sandbags back up the shaft into the horse.

Eric and Michael decided that everything would have to be speeded up if they wanted to complete their escape before winter. Certainly, the longer the tunnel became, the slower their progress, because digging the tunnel and dragging the bags of sand all the way back to the shaft was taking too much of one man's time. The

How the man in the shaft pulled the sand back from the tunnel digger.

solution was to have two men working below ground, one to dig and the other to handle the bags of sand.

To manage this they would need to recruit a third man, so that one of the escape team could always be with the vaulters. That was when Oliver Philpot joined the team.

At the same time Eric and Michael devised a novel way of

Inside the wooden horse; one man in position for being carried.

speeding up their progress and improving the air supply in the tunnel at the same time. Using a large metal basin they made a

toboggan, which slid the sand back from the tunnel face to the shaft. The constant movement of the basin to and fro greatly improved the flow of air.

This was such a vastly improved system that they decided to spend two sessions a day below ground—and that meant that the vaulters had to turn out twice a day, too.

By the end of August the

three men realised that they were in a race with time: they had to escape by the end of October at the latest, before winter set in. Early in September they reckoned that they must have dug past the perimeter fence. Eric Williams slithered along to the

end of the tunnel with a long iron poker, which he carefully pushed through to the surface. Oliver Philpot wandered along the edge of the camp until he spotted the poker sticking above the ground. They had, indeed, stretched their tunnel just past the fence.

Yet the tunnel was still not sufficiently long to enable them to make their escape. Any break would have to' be made under cover of darkness, but the powerful lamps all around the camp lit up the ground on both sides of the fence for several metres. They needed to tunnel for at least another 3-4 metres (10-13 feet). Ideally, the tunnel should be aimed to break through in a deep ditch, which would give them extra cover when they surfaced, but it was by then well into autumn. They could no longer depend on the weather being dry enough for the vaulting to continue.

Their luck held. September and October were months of beautiful Indian summer. Work on the tunnel progressed so well that they planned their escape for Friday evening, October 29. It was also decided that all three would go down into the tunnel that evening and dig the last section, burrowing their way to freedom like human moles. This would be the most dangerous part of the whole operation, because if the tunnel collapsed on them there would be no one to come to their rescue: all the other prisoners would be locked in their cells for the night.

On Friday morning, October 29, 1943 the vaulting team trotted out carrying the wooden horse with Eric Williams and Michael Codner clinging inside. Michael was wearing a black mask, made from a stocking, and a black, close-fitting costume made from a pair of long-johns dyed black. This was his escape costume. He stayed in the tunnel for the rest of the day.

Eric was carried back to the canteen inside the horse, with the usual bags of sand. On the second vaulting session that afternoon Eric went back to the tunnel with sacks filled with civilian clothes, emergency food supplies, false papers and money. He hid these in the shaft before he returned to the canteen for the last time.

Early that evening the vaulters turned out for a third session, and on that occasion the wooden horse creaked so much that all those involved in the escape plot feared it would collapse. The reason was that inside this time were three men: Eric and Oliver Philpot, both wearing their black escape costumes, and a third prisoner whose job was to seal off the top of the shaft once all three escapers were together in the tunnel.

It was 4.15 pm when Eric and Oliver joined Michael at the far end of the tunnel. For the next 75 minutes they worked feverishly digging their way towards freedom. At precisely 5.30 pm they broke through to the surface, and glimpsed a few stars in the sky as the cold October night air came sweeping in.

Half an hour later they had made the hole large enough to climb out. Their timing was perfect. For precisely on the hour all

'They slipped out of the tunnel like three black shadows . . . and ran into the forest. They were free.'

the other prisoners in the camp started an uproar—blowing bugles, singing, shouting and generally creating mayhem.

While the attention of the German guards was thus distracted, Eric Williams, Michael Codner and Oliver Philpot slipped out of the tunnel like three black shadows, ran across the last stretch of brightly floodlit ground, and disappeared into the sanctuary of the nearby pine forest. They were free.

The route to England
After they had raced clear of the tunnel the three escapers cleaned themselves up and put on their civilian clothes. Then they split up. Eric Williams and Michael Codner travelled together and Oliver Philpot went off on his own.

Eric and Michael travelled by train and boat to Denmark, where members of the underground helped them to reach Sweden, a neutral country. Oliver calmly took the train to Danzig (now Gdansk) and stowed away on a Swedish boat.

Within three weeks of their escape all three were back in Britain.

A LONG, LONG WALK

One hundred children escape the Japanese

Ai-weh-deh

The crowd of laughing, chattering children gathered around the small woman whom they knew as Ai-weh-deh, the virtuous one. She was for many of them the only mother they had ever known. Smiling back, she told them: 'Tonight I want you to go to bed early. Tomorrow we're going for a long walk across the mountains—a long, long walk!'

The children—there were almost a hundred of them—went scampering off to their quarters in the battered mission at Yangcheng. This city in the Chinese province of Shansi, about 560 kilometres (350 miles) south-east of Peking, was becoming a centre of war. The year was 1941, and World War II had just spread to Asia. But China and Japan had been at war for many years already—and now the Japanese armies were coming. As a Christian missionary, the European woman known as Ai-weh-deh was already on the Japanese 'wanted' list, and the children, too, would be in danger.

So Ai-weh-deh decided she and her little charges must escape over the mountains to Sian, where they would be safe. She had no money and no food for the journey, but the local mandarin (government official) provided some millet and two men to carry it part of the way. Sadly she looked around the mission which was her home, and the home too of the orphaned or abandoned children in her care. It was a strange mission: it was really an inn for muleteers (mule drivers, the equivalent then of long-distance truck drivers in that part

of China). And it had a strange name—the Inn of Eight Happinesses.

At dawn the next day the party set out: 27 big boys and girls, the oldest only fifteen, the rest a horde of noisy children under eight years old. They trudged slowly along the mountain trails, stopping every so often for a roll-call to ensure that no one was missing. From time to time they lit a fire and boiled up some of the millet in an iron pot. By the time each child had filled its basin there was very little left for Ai-weh-deh.

But the millet did not last for ever. The seventh day found them with no food and no shelter. Their shoes were almost worn out, and many of them had cut and bleeding feet. Just as Ai-weh-deh was wondering what to do a party of Chinese soldiers came along—and the food problem was solved for that day.

Five days later they had crossed the mountains and were stumbling, hungry and footsore, down towards the village of Yuan Ku on the Yellow River—and safety. But there was no help for them in Yuan Ku. The Japanese had bombed it, and only one old man, too old to run away, was left. They walked down to the banks of the river—but there were no boats to cross it.

For three days Ai-weh-deh and her charges waited by the river, living on a few scraps of food they found in the ruins of Yuan Ku. Then on the third day the sound of a hundred children singing a hymn attracted the attention of some more Chinese

'A big, noisy party, trudging slowly along the mountain trails.'

soldiers who were patrolling the river bank, watching for the Japanese. The soldiers signalled to their colleagues on the opposite bank, and a boat came over to take the weary party across. On the other side villagers invited them into their houses for a meal.

At the town of Mien Chih, a few kilometres further on, they were given more food—and an officious policeman wanted to arrest Ai-weh-deh for crossing the river illegally. Luckily the local mandarin came to their aid, and directed them to a train

which would take them part of their journey. For most of the children this was the most terrifying part of the whole adventure. As the huge iron dragon, breathing fire and smoke, came clanking into the station, the party of children broke and fled. It took ages to round them all up again. . . .

The train journey lasted four days. Then they had to set out on foot again, and cross another range of mountains. After walking for three days they came to another railway line. This time they were picked up by a train which was carrying coal, so the homeless refugees were wedged into coal trucks to rattle

slowly through the night. The next morning there were roars of laughter—'Ai-weh-deh, look, we've all gone black!'

Another train journey, this time in proper carriages, took them to Sian; but the city was too full to receive them. At last there was help: a refugee organisation took charge of the bedraggled party, and after a fourth train journey the children were found places in an orphanage at the city of Fufeng. Their search for a haven had taken over a month.

As for Ai-weh-deh, she collapsed with fever. Missionary doctors took charge of her and nursed her through weeks of delirium until she had recovered.

Ai-weh-deh's secret

Ai-weh-deh was the heroine of the long, long walk. But she was no ordinary heroine. For her real name was Gladys Aylward, and she was a parlourmaid from London who had used her savings to go to China and become a missionary there.

Altogether Gladys Aylward spent 20 years in China. Three years after her epic journey she returned to England, and her story came out. A film, *The Inn of the Sixth Happiness,* was made about it. Gladys spent the rest of her life in England, lecturing and preaching. She died in 1970 at the age of 68.

DOWN IN THE DESERT
Stranded pilot's survival

Roy Moffat crouched beneath the wing of his single-engine Avro aeroplane, wiped the sweat from his face and stared out across the shimmering Australian desert that stretched as far as he could see. Nothing moved out there beneath the blazing, cloudless, copper-coloured sky.

Licking his parched lips, Roy tried not to think about his growing thirst. He also tried to ignore the white towers and other buildings that could be glimpsed through the heat haze on the horizon. They almost seemed to mock his predicament. Roy had noticed them earlier that day as the intense heat increased, and knew them for what they were: only a mirage.

It was so easy to lose all track of time, stranded in the desert. Yet it was only a matter of hours, in the cool of that summer morning in 1967, since he had climbed into the Avro's cockpit and taken off from a small airport

outside Adelaide. His trip was a routine 2,580 kilometres (1,600 miles) flight across the heart of Australia to Darwin in the north. It was simple enough for such an experienced bush-pilot as Roy. And a second pilot, Chas Miller, was accompanying him in another light plane.

There should have been nothing to worry about, and there was not—until the last lap. They were flying above Australia's most desolate region, some 480 kilometres (300 miles) from Darwin, when the engine of Roy's plane suddenly cut out. Roy swiftly brought the plane under control; he glided down towards the desert, searched out the best landing place and rolled easily enough to a halt. Sliding back the cockpit, he clambered out on to the ground, and as he did so the heat waves blasted around him as hot as those from the open doors of a furnace.

Chas Miller's plane was

circling low overhead. Roy squinted up through the glare of sunlight and waved his arms to let the other pilot know he had landed safely. Chas waggled his plane's wings, signalling that he had noted Roy's position—and then flew off towards Darwin.

All that seemed so long ago to Roy as he stretched out uncomfortably beneath the Avro's shadow. He felt annoyed with himself that he had no survival kit in the Avro; it meant he had no food or water. On the other hand, he did not expect to be marooned there for too long. He

glanced ruefully at a bottle tucked into his shirt pocket. It looked like water, and he wished it were—instead of hair tonic.

All that afternoon Roy kept watching the desert for the dust cloud that would indicate a rescue party—and watching the sky for the black speck that would mean a plane was coming to collect him. But there was nothing. Nothing at all. Despite his disappointment, he was almost relieved when darkness fell and it grew cooler beneath the deep purple sky. It gave him time to think. And that was when he made an error of judgment.

Stuart Highway—nick-named 'The Bitumen'—runs across that desert from south to north. Roy thought that if he reached the highway he stood a better chance of being picked up. He took a bearing on the stars of the Southern Cross, rose to his feet and started walking in the direction of Stuart Highway. He was convinced that it could not be far away. Leaving the scene of

the landing was his first mistake. His second was believing that he could reach Stuart Highway, because it lay 115 kilometres (more than 70 miles) distant, which was too far for any man in his predicament to cover.

Roy planned to walk by night and rest by day. As the sun was rising that first morning, he saw animal tracks—several of them—all heading in the same direction. He guessed they led to a water-hole, and they did. But the supposed water-hole was simply a patch of dried mud. Sprawled in the shade of some scrub, he remembered the bottle of hair tonic. He took his first mouthful to ease his parched mouth and throat. It tasted foul. Roy rinsed the greasy mixture around his mouth and spat it out. It made him feel better. Then he crawled further into the shade to rest.

In the evening he set out again to search for Stuart High-

way, but that was when he started to lose all sense of direction. For Roy no longer had the stars to guide him. On that evening and on the next two evenings the heavens were obscured by clouds which disappeared with the following days' sunrise. Lacking food and water—for his precious store of hair tonic soon ran out—Roy Moffat became semidelirious.

Every water-hole he stumbled across proved to be nothing more than hardened, sun-dried mud. One morning rain fell. It was only a short-lived shower and at first Roy thought it was just another mirage—or that he was losing his mind. Yet it *was* rain. It was enough to soak him through and refresh him, and it gave him sufficient energy to carry on roaming the desert, looking for the elusive highway. Sometimes he thought that Chas Miller had failed to reach Darwin himself—or perhaps the search party had given up. But then he spotted a Royal Australian Air

'All that afternoon Roy kept watching the desert ... for a rescue party.'

Force Lincoln flying low and slowly across the desert. Staggering towards it, he waved his arms, danced about and yelled, but the plane carried on and on until it disappeared. On another occasion Roy glimpsed what he thought were several Aborigines crossing a small rocky outcrop. But when he reached the rocks, the men had disappeared as silently as they had come.

Roy Moffat knew that he could not continue for much longer in such conditions. The fourth day he reckoned would be his last. And then he came across the first signs that a search had been launched for him. He saw car tracks in the sand, and with them the first miracle. Lying among the tracks he found a large, fresh, shining orange. It was like a gift from the gods— the fruit must have fallen from one of the vehicles.

It was the first food he had eaten in almost five days. Roy crept wearily with the orange among some scrub. As the sun rose higher and the day became hotter, he stretched out in the shade, slowly—ever so slowly—

savouring each segment of that orange. Yet Roy knew that he could go no further.

Had Roy Moffat remained with his aeroplane, the search party would have rescued him the morning after the plane landed. Instead, trucks and jeeps had been scouring the desert for him without success.

On the very morning that Roy found the orange, the search party, led by Police-Constable Joe Gordon, was about to give up when one of them discovered a footprint in a patch of soft sand. It was a fresh print. It might have been made by a wandering Aborigine, but Constable Gordon decided to search for one more hour. The rescuers followed the line of the print, and that was how they finally discovered Roy. He was sitting hunched up, his head on his knees.

Roy stared without moving as the rescue vehicles pulled up to a stop. He still did not move as the men climbed out of the jeeps and trucks and came towards him. For a full two minutes, Roy Moffat refused to believe the evidence of his own eyes.

Triumph and tragedy

A short cut was the undoing of two great explorers, Robert O'Hara Burke and William John Wills. In February 1861, after six months' travelling, they became the first men to cross Australia from south to north, when they reached the Gulf of Carpentaria.

With two companions, John King and Charles Gray, they set out to retrace their steps to Cooper Creek, halfway back to Melbourne, where they expected to find a relief party. Gray, who was very weak, died on the journey. But when the other three reached Cooper Creek (pictured above), no one was there.

Rashly, Burke decided to take a short cut across the desert to Adelaide. For four weeks they wandered in torrid heat, helped by friendly Aborigines, but on June 28 Burke and Wills died. King, who was only 20, survived to be rescued.

I'M A DOCTOR

Saved by the saint from Devil's Island

Father Arnaiz Selles gazed out across the mist-shrouded Gulf of Paria in Venezuela and sighed in sorrow at the sight of so many corpses floating out on the tide. Beside him, two men worked wearily carrying more of the dead from the beach to the sea.

The community of Irapa was dying. Out of almost 12,000 people who had lived in the town, far more than half had died within three weeks from an epidemic of fever. Those who still survived knew that they could

expect no help, because troops had sealed off the roads leading from the Paria Peninsula, where Irapa stood. They had orders to shoot anybody trying to escape from stricken Irapa, because the Venezuclan government was determined to keep the epidemic from spreading.

Sadly, unable to believe that such callousness could exist in 1928, Father Selles closed his eyes for a few moments and prayed for a miracle. It was a prayer that received an answer

Devil's Island off French Guiana as it is today.

'The priest opened his eyes and saw a battered boat drifting towards the beach.'

immediately in an almost uncanny way.

'Father Selles—look!' One of the men shook his arm. The priest opened his eyes and saw a battered, crudely-patched open boat drifting out of the mists towards the beach.

The boat drew nearer and Father Selles saw five men sprawled in the bottom. With the help of the two Venezuelans the priest waded into the water, pulled the boat ashore and helped the five men stagger to a fire that was smouldering nearby. The priest studied them in the firelight. Although their clothes were virtually in rags, he guessed correctly that they were convicts fleeing from Devil's Island, the notorious penal colony off the coast of French Guiana. They must have made an incredible escape, because Devil's Island lay almost 1,600 kilometres (1,000 miles) along the coast from Irapa.

Suddenly, the convicts recovered and looked around them. They stared at the corpses on the beach. Without a word, four of them went back to their boat and pushed it out to sea again. But the fifth man remained. After accepting some food, he asked in French: 'What is wrong here?'

'There is an epidemic of jungle fever,' explained Father Selles. The other man said: 'I am very weak, Father, because we were 23 days at sea with little food and no water, and we went through three storms, but perhaps I can help. My name is Pierre Bougrat. I am a doctor. . .'

The miraculous fact was not just that Bougrat was a qualified doctor, but he was also a specialist in tropical diseases. After Bougrat had rested and eaten, he asked Father Selles about the sort of plants that grew around Irapa. Then he carefully described those which he thought he could use to help treat the sick.

Father Selles sent some of the townsmen off to collect leaves, plants and herbs. Soon they returned and Pierre Bougrat prepared his medicine in a pot above the fire on the beach. He then

'Eight of them forced their way through the jungle.'

instructed the priest how to prepare and administer the potion, and soon many of the people were making it themselves under the priest's supervision. Within two days the epidemic was under control. Within a week people stopped dying from the fever. Although everybody knew that Pierre Bougrat was an escaped convict, possibly guilty of murder, to the people of Irapa he quickly became their saint who had come from the sea.

Father Selles and Pierre

'Hurricanes battered the boat during its 23 days at sea.'

Bougrat talked about the convict's past life, and the priest gradually learned how the doctor was sentenced to life imprisonment on Devil's Island for the alleged murder of a patient. The voyage from Marseilles, in France, across the Atlantic to South America was not a pleasant one, manacled and with 600 other prisoners in the hold of a convict ship. Illness and disease were rampant during the voyage, but with no medicines or equipment Pierre Bougrat could do little to

fight them, He had to watch man after man dying on board the ship.

Once on Devil's Island he was appointed prison doctor—his predecessor had resigned and returned to Europe some time earlier. For three years Pierre Bougrat practised his profession with few medical tools and very little in the way of drugs, except what he could make himself. He wrote letter after letter to France claiming his innocence and asking for his case to be re-examined.

After three years Bougrat realised that his letters were making no impact at all. So when he heard that some of the prisoners were planning an escape in a boat which they had found washed up on the beach, he decided to join them. Secretly, they patched up the ramshackle vessel as best they could and gathered together a small supply of food and water. One moonless night eight of them crept from their huts, forced their way through the jungle, pushed their boat out to sea and set off northwest towards the Caribbean islands, where they hoped to find a country which would not allow the French to extradite them.

Three hurricanes battered the boat during its 23 days at sea. The mast, sail and oars were washed overboard; so were some of the supplies and three of the convicts. Eventually their water supply was reduced to handfuls of rain scooped up from the bottom of the boat. The fact that five men survived to reach Irapa was another miracle. Nobody ever discovered what happened to the four who fled from the beach that night, leaving Pierre Bougrat behind.

Normally the Venezuelan government sent all escaped convicts back to Devil's Island. When the French authorities eventually heard that Bougrat was living in Irapa, they formally requested his extradition. Father Selles, followed by hundreds of people from Irapa, walked 500 kilometres (300 miles) to the capital, Caracas, to beg the government not to return Bougrat to the penal colony. The government agreed.

It was the first time that Venezuela had ever rejected such a request from the French, but the polite refusal added: 'The people of the Paria Peninsula regard Dr Bougrat as a saint. We think he should remain among them.' When Dr Bougrat was assured that he could remain in Venezuela he settled down to practise medicine in Irapa, and to continue with his campaign by letter to establish his innocence of the murder charge against him. For he always resolutely maintained his innocence.

Pierre Bougrat died in 1962 and thousands of mourners attended his funeral. His escape from the notorious Devil's Island had succeeded beyond his wildest dreams. But he was never able to clear himself of the accusation of murder.

'Father Selles, followed by hundreds of people from Irapa, walked to the capital.'

THE ANGRY SEAS

Family survives shipwreck

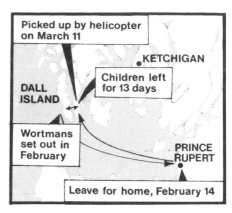

The route taken by the Wortmans in their boat.

Gigantic waves crashed down on the small schooner *Home* as a full gale sent her scuttling across the angry seas of the Gulf of Alaska. It was one of the most ferocious storms in the Gulf in living memory—and the Wortman family found themselves trapped right in the centre of it all.

Just a few days earlier, on February 14, 1979, they had set sail from Prince Rupert, British Columbia, to return to their base at Refugio, on Suemez Island, Alaska. It was a family outing for Elmo Wortman, his fifteen-year-old son Randy, and his daughters Cindy, fourteen, and Jelna, twelve—a trip of about 240 kilometres (150 miles) in the supposedly sheltered waters of the Alexander Archipelago.

Forced off course, *Home* was almost on the rocks of remote Long Island before Elmo Wortman realised the danger. Because of the driving snow he could barely see beyond the schooner's bows. He dropped a sea anchor, and started the schooner's auxiliary engine in an effort to pull back from the rocks and out to sea—and comparative safety. But the turbulent waves sent the sea anchor's cable whirling around, to become snarled up in the propeller. The engine stopped, and almost at once *Home* was aground on the rocks. Battered by the wind and heavy seas, she quickly started to break up.

Elmo, Randy, Cindy and Jelna collected as much as they could to help them survive. Wearing life-jackets and rubber boots, they thrust a small, two-seater skiff over the side, together with spare canvas for sails, some timbering, and a few mattresses. They snatched up what food they could—half-a-dozen apples, some onions and a few cartons of fruit juice. Then they too were swept overboard.

The life-jackets helped to keep them warm, but their boots were soon ripped to shreds by the rocks and washed away by the sea. But they made it to land.

Elmo Wortman was familiar with the Alaskan coast. He had sailed there many times, and believed they were not too far from Rose Inlet, on Dall Island, where his friend Pat Tolson had a trapper's cabin. So he decided to make for the cabin and seek shelter there. Elmo and Cindy clambered along the rocky shore in their stockinged feet, while Randy and Jelna paddled along in the skiff.

It took the Wortmans a whole day to reach Kaigani point, about one and a half kilometres (one mile) from where they were shipwrecked. There the weary party constructed a makeshift shelter from wooden spars and canvas, where they spent the night huddled together. Next day, with the storm still raging all around them, they worked to turn their skiff into a raft which could carry them all to Rose Inlet, 24 kilometres (fifteen miles) away up the Kaigani Strait.

Four weary days after they had set out on their raft, Elmo Wortman beached it on what he felt certain was Rose Inlet. It was in fact Keg Point, still eight kilometres (five miles) from the cabin. By now they were all at the

'Gigantic waves crashed down on the small schooner.'

point of exhaustion. Elmo knew he could not expect the two girls to face any further hazards in such weather. So he and Randy collected some timber, which had been cast up on the beach by the storm, and built a crude shelter for the girls. They were able to use their canvas and the mattresses to make it.

Then, kissing his daughters, Elmo set off with Randy on what he expected would be a round trip of a few hours. After a morning's struggle along the coast Elmo and Randy realised it has been a mistake to leave Keg Point so soon.

They were both so tired, and buffeted by the incessant wind, that they could hardly paddle the skiff through the still-rough seas. But there could be no turning back now: the wind and current were too strong.

Late that afternoon the two arrived at Rose Inlet. There they had to abandon the skiff because the sea started to freeze—not hard enough to walk on, but too much for them to drive the little boat through it. They scrambled ashore and stumbled and slithered through the snow—still only in stockinged feet. It was

dark when they reached the cabin, to find it deserted. Not only was Pat Tolson missing, but his radio transmitter was out of action, too, so they could not radio for help. But there were food, shelter, and fuel for the stove.

Elmo's plan was that they should take a brief rest, dry out, see what spare clothes Pat had left in the cabin, and then make their way back to Keg Point to collect the girls. Yet once the warmth from the stove began to thaw out their frozen limbs they suffered excruciating pains—so violent that they were almost delirious. At that moment the storm blew up with renewed violence, and thick snow began to fall. Soon Elmo and Randy were trapped inside the cabin by thick, frozen drifts.

It was March 5 before the snow thawed sufficiently for Elmo and Randy to break out of the cabin and set anxiously off for Keg Point with food and clothing for Cindy and Jelna. The journey took them nearly 30 hours. The girls had now been marooned for 13 days, and Elmo dreaded what he would find. But to his joy Cindy and Jelna were still alive, though Jelna was so weak that she had hardly been able to leave the shelter. All that had kept the girls going was a meagre diet of raw shellfish and seaweed which Cindy collected along the beach.

After a nourishing meal the girls were wrapped in warm clothing, boots and blankets, and the family set out for Pat Tolson's cabin together. This time the trapper was there—he had arrived back soon after Elmo and Randy left. His transmitter was working again, too, and at once he radioed to the US Coastguard.

On March 11, almost a month after their ordeal began, a coastguard helicopter collected the Wortman family and took them to hospital. Elmo Wortman's feet were so badly frostbitten that several toes had to be amputated. He took it philosophically: 'At least my family are still alive,' he said.

JAIL-BREAKER

The story of Jack Sheppard

Jack Sheppard

That ought to hold him, thought the jailers of London's Newgate Prison, as they eyed the young man who occupied their strongest cell, the 'Castle'. He was both manacled, and chained to the floor. For he was Jack Sheppard, whose thefts and daring escapes from jail had made him notorious by the early age of 22.

Sheppard began his career quietly enough, as a carpenter's apprentice. But in 1723, when he was 21 years old, he met his doom at a tavern in Drury Lane. Her name was Elizabeth Lyon, known better to the underworld as 'Edgeworth Bess'. Bess soon became Jack's girl friend, but she had expensive tastes, and to satisfy them Jack needed far more money than he could earn as an apprentice. So he ran away from his master, set up home with Bess, and began a life of crime.

Within a few weeks Jack was caught and locked up in St. Giles Roundhouse. In April 1724 he escaped but was recaptured almost at once with Bess. The pair were clapped into the New Prison at Clerkenwell; both escaped in May. With nothing now to lose Jack stepped up his crime rate and hardly a day passed without his robbing somebody. But what the law could not do a fellow thief did. Jonathan Wild, who was the uncrowned king of London's underworld, scented a rival in Jack, so he tipped off the authorities. Jack was arrested, and on August 13 he was tried at the Old Bailey and condemned to death.

However, Bess was free, and she and a friend named Poll Maggot helped Jack to get out of the condemned cell at Newgate. Jack

was careless. Instead of hiding, he was seen around his old haunts, and on September 10 he was back in Newgate, to face a new trial.

Visitors, however, Jack had in plenty, and soon he had a small file which he hid in a Bible. Before he could cut through his fetters he had a visit from the chaplain who picked up the Bible to make a moralising point—and out dropped the file.

A day or two later Jack had some more tools, which he hid in a chair provided for his jailers. Jack picked the locks on his fetters every evening to have a few hours with his limbs free—and was caught again when one of the jailers paid him an unexpected visit. The result was even heavier fetters.

A week of misery passed, until one of his visitors was able to leave behind a rusty nail. It was none too soon: the new court

sessions had begun, and Jack's trial was looming up. On October 14 Jack decided to make another bid for freedom. As luck would have it he had a succession of visitors—unwelcome ones, mostly prison officials.

As jailer William Austin left he said, 'I'll be too busy to come back this evening. Is there anything more you want?'

'No,' said Jack, 'but it's so lonely here in the dark—if you can't manage another visit tonight do try to come along early tomorrow morning!'

Austin promised to do so,

'He climbed up the chimney . . . to the room above.'

'Risking the noise, Jack smashed a hole in the wall and reached through to unbolt the door.'

and with a crash shut and locked the cell door. Jack was alone.

A rusty nail may not seem much of a tool, but it was strong and Jack was skilful. Within minutes he had unlocked his handcuffs and freed himself from the huge padlock that secured him to the floor. His legs remained shackled together, but Jack had enormous strength. An hour or so later the chain that joined his legs had snapped, and the loose ends were tucked inside his stockings.

'The Castle' fully deserved its name—but it had a chimney, and Jack had already decided that that was his way out. The flue had an iron bar across it to foil any such attempt, but Jack, armed with the heavy padlock, chipped at the brickwork until the bar came loose. Armed with the bar, he climbed up the chimney and broke into the room

above, which was disused. It was in complete darkness, but Jack felt his way around, picking up another nail, until he came to the door. In fifteen minutes he had picked the lock and stepped out into a passage.

There was one other door in the passage. It was bolted and led to the prison chapel. Risking the noise, Jack smashed a hole in the wall and reached through to unbolt the door. Inside the chapel another door barred his way. It was tougher still, but soon it, too, swung open.

Beyond the chapel lay another passage, another door, and the roof. So far Jack had been working for five hours, as the chimes of a nearby clock told him. This last door was even tougher, but Jack wrenched the lock off, and in a few minutes stood on the roof, breathing the fresh air.

The way was clear for him to escape, but the roofs of the houses below the prison walls were just too far away for him to jump. Coolly Jack made his way back to his cell—to fetch his blankets.

Knotting them together, he let himself down, forced an attic window, and made his way into a house. But the people there were still awake—so Jack settled down on a bed in the attic and had a quiet sleep.

Two hours later he crept downstairs and let himself out by the front door. He was free.

The last journey

Jack Sheppard never learned his lesson. A few days later he was back in his old haunts in the Drury Lane area—and on the evening of October 31 the law caught up with him, drunk as a lord in a low tavern.

This time he was watched day and night. He was tried again, condemned to death, and on November 16, 1724, he was taken to Tyburn (now Marble Arch), and hanged in front of a vast crowd.

MAN OVERBOARD

Saved in mid-Atlantic

Bill Honeywill

It was a beautiful sunny morning when Bill Honeywill woke up and decided to start swimming to Madeira. The island was more than 160 kilometres (100 miles) away, but the 28-year-old engineer had little choice in the matter. For he was floating quite alone in the vast expanse of the Atlantic Ocean.

The cruise liner *Sa Vaal*, in which he had been sailing back to England from South Africa, had long since disappeared over the horizon. It was half-past six in the morning on Friday, August 28, 1970. Bill was bobbing about in the sea—and not a soul knew he was there.

Two hours earlier Bill Honeywill was taking a last stroll around the deck of the *Sa Vaal* before going to bed. He paused to lean on the rail and savour the peacefulness of a night at sea. Then suddenly he found himself plummeting down into the water. All he remembers of the next few moments is surfacing and seeing the *Sa Vaal* sailing away from him. Then he blacked out.

Bill Honeywill was certainly a very lucky young man. For one thing, there were no sharks about, which there had been earlier in the voyage. For another, doctors claimed later that he was 'one of those people, making up about 4 per cent of the world's population, who can stay afloat in water even though they are still quite unconscious'.

Bill must have been treading water instinctively for the two hours during which he was unconscious. The next thing he remembers is that 'I woke up at daybreak and wondered what to

do. I decided just to keep myself afloat, and then started to toy with the idea of swimming to Madeira.'

At nine o'clock that morning Captain Alan Freer, skipper of the *Sa Vaal*, was told that passenger Bill Honeywill had not slept in his cabin the previous night. A search showed that the missing man was nowhere on board the 33,000-ton ship. Captain Freer ordered inquiries to be set afoot as to where and when Bill Honeywill had last been seen on board. They revealed that he must have disappeared around half-past four that morning.

Captain Freer ordered the ship to turn back on its course, towards the Canary Islands. He decided to search an area some 100 kilometres long by 15 kilometres wide (60 miles by nine miles). This was to allow for the Canary current, which could have carried the missing man away from the ship's direct route.

Anyone who has ever crossed the Atlantic, by boat or in an aeroplane, will know that looking for one man in that vast expanse of heaving water is like looking for a needle in a haystack. And there was the possibility that he had not survived, anyway.

Yet at about four o'clock that afternoon, as the *Sa Vaal* crossed and re-crossed the search area, Second Officer Alan Stewart shouted, 'Look! There he is!'

Bill Honeywill, a small speck in the grey mass of the ocean, was waving frantically at the ship he had left almost twelve hours earlier.

Describing the rescue later, Captain Freer said: 'It was fan-

'He surfaced to see the *Sa Vaal* sailing away from him.'

tastic. There he was, swimming through the ocean towards us, waving his arms and shouting. We threw out a marker buoy while we slowed down the ship, then launched a lifeboat. And as the crew helped Mr. Honeywill out of the water, his first words were: "It's been a nice day for a swim."'

Bill Honeywill was bruised by the impact of his fall into the water. He was suffering from exhaustion, cramp, sunburn and general exposure. But he had established a new world record: nobody else had ever survived for as long as he had swimming about in the open sea.

When he was recovering in hospital in England, Bill Honeywill said: 'I'm not surprised I'm still alive.'

The reason for his confidence in his ability to survive might well have been because, just before he left Africa, he had had his fortune told by an African witch-doctor in Lesotho.

The prediction was: 'You will not die violently. You'll live to an old age.'

Sleepdiver!

Uwe Klante was a man overboard with a difference: he dived into the sea in the middle of the night while sleepwalking. During a Baltic cruise aboard the German freighter *Marie Both* on June 10, 1966 he awoke to find himself only a few hundred metres from a navigation buoy. He swam to it, and clung there for nearly six hours until a passing ship picked him up.

DEAD OR ALIVE

Churchill's escape in the Boer War

Winston Churchill during his Boer War adventures.

A group of British prisoners at Pretoria. Churchill is standing on the far right.

The handwritten notice posted outside Government House, Pretoria, was uncompromising: '£25 reward is offered . . . to anyone who brings the escaped prisoner of war Churchill dead or alive to this office.'

It was the latest episode in the already adventurous life of 24-year-old Winston Churchill, son of a former British Cabinet Minister and grandson of the seventh Duke of Marlborough.

The year was 1899, and the Boer War between the British and the Boer (Dutch) settlers in South Africa had been fought fiercely for several weeks.

Churchill, a former Army officer, was in South Africa as a special correspondent for a London newspaper, the *Morning Post*. An old friend, Captain Aylmer Haldane, had invited him to join an armoured train on patrol up the railway line towards Lady-

£25

(twenty-five pounds sterling)

REWARD

is offered by the Sub-Commission
of the Fifth Division, on behalf of
Special Constable of the said division
to anyone who brings the escaped
prisoner of war

CHURCHILL,

dead or alive to this office.
For the Sub-Commission of the
Fifth Division.

LODK. de HAAS, sec.

The Boer proclamation which offered £25 'dead or alive' for Churchill's capture. Inset is the original text in Afrikaans.

smith, which was besieged by the Boers. Suddenly the train came under fire, and three of its wagons were derailed. Churchill volunteered to try to get the engine clear, and succeeded after an hour's work under fire. The locomotive, laden with wounded men, retreated down the line; Churchill and Captain Haldane, with some other British soldiers, were taken prisoner.

The captives were marched for two days across country in drenching rain to a railway station, and were then taken by train to Pretoria and locked up in the State Model Schools, which the Boers were using as a prisoner-of-war camp. Churchill claimed that he was a civilian and the Boers should therefore release him; but they refused to

do so. On November 30 Churchill celebrated his 25th birthday—in captivity.

Churchill, Haldane and another man began plotting to escape. The easiest route was by way of an outbuilding near the high wall around the school. The school compound was brilliantly lit and guarded by sentries. On the evening of December 12 the other two tried to escape, but could not dodge the sentries. Then Churchill decided to try his luck. While he hid in the outbuilding two of the sentries paused in their keen vigil for a quick chat.

'Now or never!' Churchill told himself, and climbed over the wall. There he waited for his friends to join him. Then he heard another officer saying 'It's all up.' He was free, but alone—and his

colleagues had the only map and compass. In his pockets were £75, and four slabs of chocolate. He did not know the country, nor could he speak the Boer language, Afrikaans, or any of the local African languages.

But Churchill had two advantages more valuable to a man on the run: courage and audacity. He was wearing a brown flannel suit and he had a broad hat pulled down to hide his face. Humming a tune, Churchill strolled through the streets of Pretoria until he came to the railway. He decided to follow the line, so plodded on through the night. Then he heard a train starting up from the station at Pretoria; he decided that he would board it.

As the train lumbered past, gathering speed, Churchill ran, sprang, was whirled off his feet as he clung to a handhold—and found himself sitting on the couplings of a truck. He was on an

'Churchill leaped from the train into a ditch.'

empty coal train, returning to the colliery. Burrowing down among the coal sacks in the truck, Churchill made himself comfortable and went to sleep.

He woke before dawn and thought it would be as well if he left the train. Although it was moving at a fair speed he leaped into the darkness, landing in a ditch shaken but unhurt. After a long drink at a nearby pool, Churchill hid for the day in a grove of trees, his only companion a large and interested vulture. His plan was to board another train the next night, but no trains came along. But there were distant lights. Might they be a Kaffir *kraal*—a native village? The Kaffirs were said to be friendly to the British. Abandoning the rail-

way, Churchill set out to walk towards the distant lights.

The journey took him most of the night. When he reached the lights he found that his objective was a coal mine. What could he do? Churchill recollected that a number of Englishmen were to be found at these mines, retained by the Boers to keep operations running. In any case, if the people were Boers or Boer sympathisers, he could always see what a large bribe could do. The alternative was wandering alone for days, with the risk of dying from hunger and thirst at least as great as recapture. Here at least there was a house—and a chance.

Churchill stepped out of the shadows, and knocked at the door of the house.

Fortune was on his side. The occupant of the house was Mr John Howard, manager of the Transvaal Collieries. When Churchill made himself known, Howard exclaimed: 'Thank God you have come here! It's the only house for twenty miles where you would not have been handed over.'

Howard gave Churchill a good meal, and then with the aid of some of the miners took him down the pit. There, in an underground gallery where there was plenty of fresh air, they made him comfortable with a mattress, blankets, a couple of candles, a bottle of whisky and a box of cigars.

Churchill spent several days in the mine, his only companions a horde of timid but ubiquitous white rats with pink eyes. Then Howard allowed him to come up to the surface and hide in the back room of the mine office. Meanwhile Howard made plans to get his visitor away. Three nights later Churchill was led down to a railway siding. There he crawled into a space which had been left in a truck laden with bales of wool. He had been provided with food, some bottles of cold tea—and a revolver.

The train was bound for the Portuguese port of Lourenço Marques (now Maputo), in Mozambique. The consignment of wool was owned by a Dutchman who was friendly to the British. He travelled with it, and by a few judicious bribes succeeded in getting the wool truck across the frontier without its being searched by the Boers.

That journey was scheduled to last sixteen hours. It took three long days, but at last Churchill saw through a peephole in the side of the truck that he was over the frontier. By the time the train at last rumbled into the station at Lourenço Marques he had tidied up all traces of his stay in the wool truck. After the train had stopped he slipped out to mingle with the crowd of loafers in the station yard, and when no one was looking he slid through the gates into the street. The Dutchman who owned the wool was waiting, and he led the way to the British Consulate.

There Churchill received a warm welcome from the secretary: 'Be off with you,' he said, 'the Consul cannot see you today. Come to his office at nine o'clock tomorrow if you want anything!'

A hero's welcome

Churchill made such a fuss that he was not kept waiting long at the British Consulate in Lourenço Marques. That evening, well fed and with a change of clothes, he was aboard a steamer bound for Durban, a British-controlled port in South Africa.

He arrived in Durban to a hero's welcome, and by Christmas Eve he was once more in the front line. But this time, since the Boers would not regard him as a civilian, he was in uniform as a lieutenant in the South African Light Horse.

Churchill went on to have a distinguished political career. He led his country as Prime Minister in the dark days of World War II.

'He spent several days in the mine, his only companions a horde of white rats.'

ESCAPE IN JAIL

Man survives the Mont Pelée disaster

The cell at St. Pierre jail.

'A glowing cloud of gas, steam and white-hot fragments of rock shot sideways . . . in just three minutes St. Pierre died.'

Auguste Ciparis was looking forward to breakfast on the morning of May 8, 1902. It was perhaps all that he had to look forward to, the next meal, and the one after that, and then—who knows? For Ciparis was under sentence of death for the crime of murder.

The 25-year-old Negro stevedore was far from comfortable. For in the city of St. Pierre, on the island of Martinique in the West Indies, the condemned cell was particularly unpleasant. It had been built on the side of the local jail, and was designed to make sure no one escaped. The walls were very thick. There was no window. The door was solid and so low that a person had to get down on hands and knees to pass through it. Over the door was a small aperture, protected by a heavy iron grating. What little air there was came in through that small hole, together with a little light.

Suddenly even that small amount of light vanished. A blast of heat, like that from a furnace door, surged through the grating, while there was a terrific crash on the roof of the cell. Ciparis threw himself on the floor, his head buried in his arms, and tried not to breathe the fumes that came with the heat. Then the heat went away, leaving Ciparis in total darkness. He was badly burned, but strangely enough only on those parts of his body that had been protected by his clothing. His hands, feet and face were untouched.

For four long days and nights Ciparis sat in his cell, suffering agonies with his burns, and without either food or water. For a while he called for help, but no one came. After a time he stopped shouting. He was too weak. Then he heard voices, and called out again. His cries were heard, and after some time the door swung open and Ciparis crawled out—to an unimaginable scene of devastation.

Of the beautiful city of St. Pierre, which had borne the title 'the Paris of the West Indies', only the condemned cell was still standing. The frightful crash was the sound of the jail falling on top of it. And of the 30,000 people who had been living in the city, only Ciparis and one other man survived.

St. Pierre had been wiped off the map by its dangerous neighbour, the volcano Mont Pelée. Few people thought of the mountain as dangerous. It rumbled and puffed occasionally, and in 1851 there was a small eruption. But nothing to worry about. People used to picnic on the shores of a lake in its crater.

Mont Pelée began to wake up in May 1901, when a small jet of steam started to blow on the edge of the lake. The following April more vents appeared, blowing out steam. On April 23 there were three deep, rumbling explosions, and crockery rattled on the shelves in St. Pierre. That was the danger signal.

From then on the mountain was in constant turmoil. A new lake formed near the top, and ash began to fall on the city, at first in a fine cloud, and then in a steady

downpour. It smelled strongly of sulphur. People stayed indoors as much as possible. Schools and shops closed. On May 5 the mountain claimed its first victims. A stream of boiling mud shot down one side, overwhelming a sugar mill. Forty workers there were buried alive.

Now comes the incredible part of the story. The Governor of Martinique, Louis Mouttet, came to the city to see for himself what

was happening. And his response to appeals for the city to be evacuated was to station troops on the roads around it to stop people leaving. The newspapers appealed for calm. A professor was quoted as saying there was no cause for alarm—people could safely stay there.

The reason for this action was political. Elections were coming up on May 10, and Mouttet was anxious to keep the voters at home until they had given him their support at the polls.

The elections were never held. The rumblings grew, the rain of ash continued, smoke and flames belched from the summit of the mountain. Then, at 7.52 on the morning of Thursday, May 8, Mont Pelée blew up. The greatest force of the blast came out of the side of the mountain.

It was as if a flame gun of gargantuan size had been trained on the town. A glowing cloud of gas, steam and white-hot fragments of rock shot sideways at a speed of nearly 290 kph (180 mph). In just three minutes St. Pierre died. The cloud passed on, leaving nothing but ruins, looking like a huge archaeological site. In that moment the fearsome heat turned thick beams to charcoal. There was no oxygen in the cloud, and no fire—but when it passed and the air returned the whole scorched and superheated city burst into flames. All but one of the ships in the harbour were also overcome.

The other survivor of the Mont Pelée disaster was a 28-year-old Negro shoemaker, Léon Compère-Léandre. He was sitting on the doorstep of his house when the final blast came. He stumbled indoors and collapsed. Everyone around him died from the fumes and heat as he watched, even those in the same room. By some miracle, Compère-Léandre must have held his breath, for his lungs were untouched.